NARRATIVE THERAPY APPROACHES FOR PHYSICAL HEALTH PROBLEMS

NARRATIVE THERAPY APPROACHES FOR PHYSICAL HEALTH PROBLEMS
Facilitating Preferred Change

Edited by
Lincoln Simmonds
and
Louise Mozo-Dutton

Routledge
Taylor & Francis Group

LONDON AND NEW YORK

First published 2018
by Routledge
2 Park Square, Milton Park, Abingdon, Oxon OX14 4RN

and by Routledge
711 Third Avenue, New York, NY 10017

Routledge is an imprint of the Taylor & Francis Group, an informa business

British Library Cataloguing-in-Publication Data
A catalogue record for this book is available from the British Library

Library of Congress Cataloging-in-Publication Data
A catalog record has been requested for this book

ISBN: 978-1-78220-276-9 (pbk)

Typeset in Palatino Linotype
by V Publishing Solutions Pvt Ltd., Chennai, India

CONTENTS

ABOUT THE EDITORS AND CONTRIBUTORS

Louise Mozo-Dutton is a clinical psychologist who works with people living with physical health conditions, an interest sparked during her training and one that has continued to grow and develop since qualifying in 2009. To date, Louise has worked within HIV services and acute in-patient medicine; she also has experience of supporting people with diabetes, stroke, multiple sclerosis, respiratory problems, and degenerative conditions. Narrative therapy remains her guiding therapeutic model; she completed the diploma in 2014 and has been part of a narrative supervision group for a number of years. She loves the way narrative conversations open up therapeutic space and possibilities, and finds this way of working incredibly hopeful, respectful, and invigorating. It is an approach in keeping with her own personal values about working with people and the problems that can be experienced.

Jennifer Pomfret is a clinical psychologist who currently works with adults with chronic fatigue syndrome and also people with infectious diseases, working with patients with HIV. She first became aware of narrative ways of working during her first assistant psychology position in Child and Adolescent Mental Health Services, working alongside children to co-construct stories, and she found the approach to be incredibly beneficial. Jennifer completed her thesis on the "Narratives of Living Well with Cystic Fibrosis", which was an inspirational journey for her. She expresses her gratitude to the patients who allowed her the opportunity to hear their stories.

Lincoln Simmonds is a clinical psychologist who is passionate about using ideas from narrative therapy in his work with children and young people. He has worked with young people with a range of physical health problems, and more recently with young people with neuromuscular difficulties. He has presented workshops, supervised other practitioners, and written about using narrative therapy approaches. Many of the ideas in this book have been derived from conversations that have looked at the application of narrative therapy ideas within health contexts, and he is extremely grateful to the co-editor of this book and facilitators of peer supervision groups and workshops he has attended, who have invariably been willing and enthusiastic in discussions. He has always been amazed at the renewed hope, and increasing sense of authorship in his own and other's lives during the course of journeys of lived experience as described by narrative therapy.

Rachel Skippon is a clinical psychologist who has worked in a range of settings spanning adult mental health, forensic services, and chronic pain. She is committed to using narrative approaches in her work, particularly valuing the collaborative nature and accessibility they provide for those who consult with her. Rachel enjoys using narrative approaches both with those using services and with colleagues and teams providing such services. Rachel is passionate about sharing the possibilities that narrative approaches can offer, especially in the context of multi-disciplinary teams and with people for whom narrative approaches are new. She hopes this book will support both aims.

Rob Whittaker is a consultant clinical psychologist and clinical lead for diabetes and HIV services at Bradford Teaching Hospitals Foundation NHS Trust in West Yorkshire, where he first worked as a hospital porter in 1991. He is particularly interested in collaborative, narrative, and social constructionist approaches to supporting people living with chronic illnesses and their healthcare teams. He also works with gender non-conforming children and their families in the Gender Identity Development Service at the Tavistock and Portman NHS Foundation

Trust. Narrative practice fits both with his love of theory and his commitment to social justice. He teaches narrative ideas at Leeds University and for the Institute of Narrative Therapy. When not working, he loves good coffee, pale ale, and the chaos of his young family.

FOREWORD

It is with great pleasure that I write a foreword for this book. Lincoln Simmonds and Louise Mozo-Dutton have been part of my narrative life for many years now, starting with meetings we held in a room up a spiral staircase in a tower at the University of Manchester too many years ago to have any record of it on my computer! I have also been involved in teaching Rachel Skippon, Rob Whittaker, and Jennifer Pomfret. Four of them have been members of the narrative supervision group in Manchester that I facilitate. So although I have had nothing to do with the direct production of this book, I feel that it reflects something of my own commitment to developing narrative therapy and to supporting narrative practitioners. As I look forward to a time when I may retire, this book confirms that there is a younger generation of narrativists who are working on the same project of developing and spreading narrative ideas. I know that narrative therapy will continue to spread and to thrive in their hands!

Narrative practice has proved to be particularly helpful in the realm of physical health, in situations where perhaps the physical realities of life may not change but where the stories that we tell and that are told about us are available for revision. This book provides theoretical and practice ideas that will be a significant contribution to the field and will inspire many others who are working in physical health to turn to narrative practice.

I know that editing a book such as this is not easy work, so my congratulations to Lincoln and Louise (and to all the contributors) on this landmark achievement!

Hugh Fox

NOTE ABOUT CASE STUDIES

There are a number of case studies used throughout this book. The case studies bring the theory and ideas into life, and hopefully serve as good examples of how to implement narrative therapy into your practice. The case examples are examples from the chapter authors' work with people or (on occasion) purely fictional. All of the real examples used have been given with the person's explicit permission, and every effort has been made to protect personal details and identity. The fictional examples are simply that: fiction, and any resemblance to any person's experiences are purely coincidental.

INTRODUCTION

Louise Mozo-Dutton and Lincoln Simmonds

The cards were laid out on the table before Anna; each one had a different phrase written on it:

Gives me time to think
Really gets me down
Hard to do homework
I don't have to do P.E. —Yayyy!
Get fed up because I can't do sleepovers
My friends get to do a lot more than I do
Makes me feel like I'll never get better
My doctor doesn't want to help me

The therapist looked up at Anna, and asked: "What would be most important to talk about first?"

The narration of an illness or diagnosis can be manifold, with an infinite number of possible stories about a person's relationship to their acute or persistent physical health problem. Thus this book is about exploring how a person wishes to live her life and view her identity within the context of "ill-health" and, throughout, we (Lincoln & Louise) find ourselves continually returning to the theme that there is no *one* or best way to do this. Instead, the narrative therapist aims to facilitate the "storying" of a person's lived experience, with the person as co-author and chief editor. The person's own personal narratives are drawn on, and great emphasis placed on what she considers to be important. Time and time again, this process has been found to create opportunities for a person to connect or reconnect with what she gives value to and hopes for in life, even whilst being affected by a physical health problem. The process is also frequently found to be invigorating for the therapist, supporting reflection and clarification of personal principles, and encouraging professional practice in keeping with these.

Why did we decide to write this book?

This book has been generated from the editors' and authors' experience of working within physical health contexts. Throughout training and post-qualifying practice, most therapists will find themselves exposed to multiple models and ways of working. However, it is narrative ideas that we have always found ourselves returning to when feeling stuck and uncertain. It is an approach that chimes with personal values in that it is deeply respectful, and acknowledging of the knowledge and skills that people possess. It can be creative, playful, and fun, yet without dismissing or minimising the seriousness of the concerns brought to the therapy room. It is an approach that expands possibilities.

In the early stages of this text, frequent conversations were had about how these ideas could be used within the field of physical health. What we found was that while some transferred over easily, others seemed to require some tweaking or special consideration. This book is therefore the sum of these discussions, and concerns the application of theory to practice, but also how practice can drive the modification of theoretical ideas. Thus, it hopes to provide a broad overview of the use of different ideas from narrative therapy, across the lifespan, and in a variety of physical health settings and formats.

Many people reading this text may not necessarily identify as "narrative therapists". This is not a problem, as the intention behind this volume is simply to encourage practitioners to have a go. Each chapter therefore endeavours to add something to the therapist's "tool kit". It might be that the person wishes to use these ideas in part, or in conjunction with another model—whatever works for them and the person with whom they are meeting. However, the reader is encouraged to remain mindful of the philosophy on which narrative therapy is based, as this can support decisions made about what to use and in what way.

What will this book cover?

There are eight sections in this book. The Introduction is concerned with familiarising the reader about the main principles of narrative therapy, and will briefly outline the philosophy that informs this approach, key overarching intentions, alongside available research.

Chapter One looks at how problems can be understood and viewed from a narrative perspective. Various ideas will be covered, including externalising that aims to assist the reader in exploring the effects and influence of a problem, but also the *person's* influence over the problem. Thinking about problems in this way supports the belief that action is always possible and likely already taking place.

Problem exploration lays the foundation for re-authoring conversations, covered in Chapter Two, whereby the focus shifts to the development of multiple stories that lie outside of, or in contrast to, the problem account. Entry points to alternative conversations are discussed, alongside ways in which preferred stories can be made visible and available to a person and their medical team.

Chapter Three examines dominant societal narratives about illness, and how such discourse can shape and influence personal stories. It considers broader stories told, for example, about how to live life "well" or to "successfully" cope with a physical health concern; in addition to thinking about how to examine, name, and deconstruct these ideas within the therapy room.

Chapter Four explores using narrative ideas with children and young people. It largely focuses on ways of supporting conversations, and presents ideas for how to do this that ensure a young person's knowledges and skills are privileged. Challenges as well as opportunities for creative clinical practice are discussed.

Chapter Five is dedicated to applying these ideas to in-patient settings. This chapter aims to bring the reader's attention to dilemmas that can arise here, and while it does not promise solutions, options and possibilities for progress are reflected upon.

Chapter Six considers ways of working with other professionals: carrying out consultation, delivering staff training, and involvement in service development. Within physical health contexts, therapists often need to think about working and consulting with the medical teams that support people.

Finally, Chapter Seven discusses the creative use of documentation within physical health contexts. Documents are an incredibly important tool when it comes to signifying preferred ways of living. However, their use also brings a unique set of responsibilities that benefit from consideration.

This text has intentionally tried to consider ways of working across the lifespan, and will draw on examples from an array of physical health settings, with a variety of people and with a range of differing presenting concerns.

Who is this book for?

This book is aimed at therapists of any profession and at any stage of their training, who would like to learn more about narrative therapy and how it can be used within their work. It is likely that the reader will have some introductory knowledge, although this does not have to be the case. Earlier chapters are focused on introducing the building blocks of this approach: core concepts, principles, and assumptions. While the later chapters think more about how these ideas can be used within specific contexts or with particular groups of people.

How is the book set up?

This book is intended to be a practical text, with each chapter covering both theory and the clinical application of ideas. We hope that the text is brought to life by the stories of people with whom we have worked. These are people who have been kind enough to allow us to use some parts of their lived experience. You may notice that each chapter has a slightly different voice depending on the author, or authors, who have written it; this reflects the varying experiences and writing styles of the contributors. There is a Glossary of key words to be found at the end of the book.

A note about maps

There are a number of worked examples of using maps within the book, although detailed descriptions of *all* the maps have not been included.

For further reading, Michael White's *Maps of Narrative Practice* (2005) provides a fantastic overview. However, as a therapist, it is still possible to engage in narrative ideas, and have narrative-informed conversations, without using one. Indeed, it is our belief that keeping in touch with the key principles and general "spirit" of the approach is more important than learning the specific categories of each and every therapeutic map. The latter remains incredibly helpful, and we would not wish to dissuade anyone from doing so. Yet the "narrative spirit" is arguably a broader compass in terms of re-orientating practice when feeling stuck or lost in work with clients.

Key principles of narrative therapy

This next section aims to introduce several of the core building blocks within narrative therapy. It is important that the reader has a basic awareness of these ideas, which will be expanded on and developed throughout the book, for it is this philosophical position that tends to mark it as different from many other therapeutic models.

Philosophy underpinning the narrative approach

"Narrative therapy was not developed from psychological discourse, but is a synthesis of the work of several social theorists including Foucault and is philosophically grounded in post-struturalism" (Besley, 2002, p. 126).

As noted by Besley, there are a great many philosophers and thinkers who have influenced and shaped the practice referred to as narrative therapy by White and Epston, from the late 1980s onwards. These include Anderson, Bruner, Bateson, Deleuze, Derrida, Foucault, Myerhoff, Geertz, Goffman, Gergen, Tomm, and Vygotsky, to name but a few. To try to summarise their influence would go beyond the scope of this section, but if you would like to read more about the evolution of this approach, papers written by Anderson (2003), Beels (2009), and Denborough (2009) provide interesting starting points. Instead, we would like to draw your attention to four key ideas within narrative therapy practice:

- reality and truth as social constructions;
- language as the means by which meaning is created;

- meaning made, bound up with issues of power and privilege;
- narrative practice as a therapy that aligns itself with non-structuralist theories of identity.

Reality and truth as social constructions

In the 1960s and 1970s, the social sciences underwent a shift in thinking known as the "interpretative turn" (White, 2004). This term was used to describe movement away from internal state theories of "self" to those that "placed [meaning] firmly at the centre of social enquiry" (White, 2004, p. 74). Rather than attempting to define and measure "essences" believed to be at the "core of personhood" (White, 2004, p. 73), interpretive theories focused on the perceived "social construction of people's realities" (White, 2004, p. 74). As White summarises:

> These were realities that were not radically derived through one's own independent construction of the events of one's life. These realities were not the outcome of some privileged access to the world as it is. They were not arrived at through some objective grasp of the nature of things. Rather, people's realities were understood to be … historical and social products, negotiated in and between communities of people and distributed throughout these communities.
>
> (White, 2004, p. 74)

Hence the idea that perceptions of reality are developed by the interactions, communications, and experiences that people have with one another and society more broadly, as opposed to being solely due to internal processes and structures. This shift in thinking signalled the dawn of social constructionism.

The role of language

The social construction of our realities is thought primarily to occur through language, as it is through words together with associated symbols, expressions, and imagery that people develop and interpret meaning. Language also allows objects, feelings, experiences, and information to be compared against one another, contrasted, and categorised. Differentiation and the practice of naming largely support this process, but can also be seen to link to wider issues relating to power and privilege. For example, why is it that one person or group is able to decide what something is to be called? What it is? Or the level of importance that should be attached to it? Historically, it has been those who occupy privileged positions who are able to participate in naming practices. Or rather, they have had their naming practices better supported by society, and thus seemingly have more power to validate some ways of living over others. Foucault (1980), in his reflections on modern power, argued that when particular understandings go on to assume a truth-like status or be perceived as common sense, they carry the capacity to shape and influence lives, as they provide a point against which people judge and measure themselves.

Structuralism and non-structuralism

Ideas of modernism translated to studies of human behaviour, with theories developed that described man as a series of drives, needs, or particular core structures (Eysenck & Eysenck, 1975). This ideology of structuralism asserted that, with careful investigation, such "traits" could be discovered, measured, and categorised for the prediction of future behaviour or distress.

Alternatively, however, if the view is taken that it is through language that a person's sense of self is constructed, and actions and experiences given meaning, then this is a process that has to occur *between people*. Concerns, worries, and fears therefore become something that are not located *within people*, but rather may be better understood as co-created constructs. This is referred to as "non-structuralism", whereby emphasis is placed on a person's intentions, purposes, wishes, values, hopes, principles, and commitments, as opposed to drives, traits, needs, defence mechanisms, unconscious motives, and natural aptitudes (Fox, 2008).

This is the philosophy on which narrative therapy is built; an approach that might even be viewed as a response or protest against structuralist ideas of self and distress. It is an alternative way of understanding that offers possibilities and reconnects with the knowledge that people are active agents within their own lives. Where problems are believed inherent, the focus tends to shift to looking to someone else, often considered more expert, to try to ameliorate concerns: opportunities for change also tend to reduce.

Narrative therapy, in contrast, believes that there are always options to respond to or interpret a situation differently, and that it is the person themselves who possesses the greatest knowledge of what works and for what reasons. Thus, key messages within the approach include:

- Stories actively shape lives and have real effects; they are not mere descriptions of life.
- The person is not the problem; the problem is the problem.
- Problems are not located within people, but rather are actively constructed between them.
- Wider discourses shape what is considered important or what people/society choose to hold themselves accountable to.
- People know a great deal about their problems and how to respond, but problems can work to separate them from this knowledge.
- The actions that each person takes tend to be underpinned by what they give value to.
- Identity is a social achievement, created in relationship with others.
- People are multi-storied: one story will only ever be a partial description of lives and identities.

Given this, the role for the narrative-informed therapist is to:

- Support a person to remember what they know, which may include what they know about how to live with, survive, manage, or respond to a problem.
- Support a person to find ways to make the problem (as defined by them) less influential in their life.
- Support a person to put into words what they value, consider precious, or how they wish to go on in life.
- Support a person to reconnect with people, ideas, knowledges that fit better with their hopes for their lives.
- Support a person to build contexts around them that sustain them. Contexts that are acknowledging of preferred accounts of life and identity.
- Support a person to link with others. Problems can work to separate people from one another, and therefore, considerable emphasis is given to (re)building networks and relationships.

So, in brief, what are narrative approaches trying to do?

The narrative therapist endeavours to assist the person to reconnect with, or become more aware of, aspects of their life, relationships, and living that may have been less available or "visible" to them. This process will tend to lead to the opening of reflective space and possibilities for the person and their life. The therapist can then work to support the active stepping back, clarification, and evaluation of information. This alongside encouragement and choice as to how the person wishes to "position" themselves in relation to these possibilities.

Thus to summarise, narrative therapy is broadly considered to have two principle aims:

One: Making visible

- To support a person to become clearer about the concerns within their life, and how those concerns affect them/others.
- To become clearer about the ideas that might contribute to the concerns or keep them going.
- To become clearer about what matters most to the person, and how they wish to go in life. As well as what (or who) can help them do this.

Two: Positioning

- By becoming clearer about these points, a person can be invited to take a position in relation to their expressed concerns and hopes, and decide;
- what fits and what does not, with how they would like to go on in life;
- what steps or actions they would like to take to lead a life more in keeping with their values and preferred ways of living.

How can narrative ideas be used in therapists' work with people?

There are two practices considered essential "must haves" in any narrative therapist's toolkit, both supporting the shaping of narrative therapy conversations. The first refers to "de-centred practice", and the second to the process of "scaffolding".

De-centred practice

In 2005, White outlined four therapeutic postures that a practitioner may assume during conversations with people. These were:

De-centred and influential (potentially invigorating of therapist)	Centred and influential (potentially burdening of therapist)
De-centred and non-influential (potentially invalidating of therapist)	Centred and non-influential (potentially exhausting of therapist)

Figure A. The four therapeutic postures (White, 2005, p. 9).

White was of the view that it was the de-centred and influential posture that was of most use to therapists, clarifying that "decentred does not refer to the intensity of the therapist's engagement (emotional or otherwise) with people seeking consultation", but rather "to the therapist's achievement in according priority to the personal stories and to the knowledges and skills of these people" (White, 2005, p. 9). Thus the de-centred posture is the position from which therapists ensure that the content of conversations are focused primarily on the person and their stories, and that it is only their knowledge and ideas that are centred. Yet therapists are not mere listeners who encourage the simple retelling of stories, but rather the re-telling of stories in a particular way. This is an active process, hence it is referred to as "influential"—not in the sense that it imposes an agenda or delivers interventions. Rather, Michael White defined influential as building a scaffold through questions and reflections which makes it possible for people to participate in exploratory conversations. Although White acknowledged that therapists will inevitably move between the described postures, he considered it most helpful to endeavour to adopt a de-centred but influential way of working, wherever possible.

Scaffolding and scaffolding distance

The therapist will often find that conversations move from "what is known and familiar" to a person to "what is possible for them to know" during the course of therapy, and they can help facilitate this process by carefully scaffolding conversations. The concept of scaffolding comes from Vygotsky (1986), who emphasised that any learning must take place within the "zone of proximal development". This means that any steps taken must be big enough to actually constitute a jump away from what the person knows already, yet small enough to ensure that it feels like a step that they can actually manage.

Vygotsky considered the scaffolding process to predominately occur with the help of others. For example, one of the authors attended a sugar-craft course. If, on arrival, the instructor had pulled out a fully furnished cake complete with various icings and patterns and simply told the attendees to copy it, then the class would have struggled to know what to do. Instead, the instructor carefully took the group through each step of the cake-making process from learning how to cut and assemble it through to making the right consistency in icing, piping, and decorative skills. By demonstrating and supporting the class in this manner, the instructor ensured that everyone was able to manage each stage before moving onto the next.

As aforementioned, there are a number of maps of narrative practice that have been developed and made available for practitioners to use, and such maps might more broadly be viewed as a way of scaffolding conversations. It would be forgivable to assume that this process is a way of "doing" narrative therapy to a person. One in which the therapist leads or instructs the person from their conceptualisation of the problem, towards explanations and understandings that are in some way better. White (2007), in contrast, believed that maps simply support conversations about the problems people experience, and help facilitate movement in a general direction. The categories of questions within them, therefore, are intended to be used more as a directional compass rather than plotting any specific pathway.

When narrative therapy is embarked upon *with* a person, the specific route of the conversations, or where they will end up, can never be known, only the general direction of travel. It is not the therapist who decides the route or path taken on this journey, but rather the person. Narrative therapy places great emphasis on this point.

Narrative therapy and research

The final section of this chapter looks to inform the reader about the evidence base for the narrative approach, although the term "evidence base" is neither neutral nor value-free. It is a construct that has been developed within a particular context, and one that acknowledges and authenticates certain understandings.

Guidance issued by the National Institute of Clinical Excellence (NICE) is informed by the medical model discourse, which postulates the idea that there are specific treatments or responses that work best for specific conditions. In order to identify these, one has to first diagnose the condition. These assumptions have been thought to map readily onto the topic of human distress. Thus, similar to physical health problems, NICE considers there to be different types of diagnosable distress and, by differentiating between them, it is believed that (perceived distinct) concerns may be more responsive to particular approaches. Identifying which techniques are thought to work best comes under the umbrella of "evidence-based".

In drawing your attention to this issue, we would not wish to suggest that this approach does not have its merits, although it does highlight that the term itself encapsulates a particular framework of understanding. Narrative therapy at times questions the rationale of wholesale, advocating that only particular types of research and experience (those seen to meet specific criteria) count as evidence, and should universally guide how people are treated (see Druker, 2014; Strong, 2012). Of course, such a position may lead to a challenge to the legitimacy of narrative therapy, as a valid and effective way of working.

In current times, and as with many other types of service, those that attend to the psychological wellbeing of people appear to be under increasing pressure, with rising demand yet reducing monies and/ or staff available. This, together with several key documents and initiatives, as highlighted by Weatherhead and Jones (2008), such as the Layard Report (2005), New Ways of Working (2007), and payment by results, have focused services on how they can get the most for their money, and ensure that practitioners' ways of working are effective. These ideas are in keeping with a business discourse, and understandably this has raised the profile of evidence and of becoming clearer about what works and for whom.

Thus, the particular challenge for narrative therapy is to "produce evidence that fits within the philosophy on which it is built, whilst evidencing its efficacy within the dominant scientific narrative" (Weatherhead & Jones, 2008, p. 38). Should the narrative community opt not to do so, Weatherhead and Jones raise the concern that this approach, alongside others more aligned with social constructionist ideas, risk "potential marginalisation" (Weatherhead & Jones, 2008, p. 98).

Standardised assessment tools remain another important issue, as such measures are often considered a central component of trials viewed as scientific; yet their development are based on philosophical principles generally thought to stand outside of narrative ideas and practice (Weatherhead & Jones, 2008). For example, criticisms levied at their use include the perceived "failure to separate a person from the problem within the language of standardised measures; the importance of co-constructing individualised narratives outside of narrow descriptions [and] the assumption of a homogeneous preferred narrative across all persons within a particular difficulty" (Weatherhead & Jones, 2008, p. 38). Weatherhead and Jones go on to think about possible ways to evidence change that are in keeping with both narrative principles and dominant models of good evidence. They did not reach a clear conclusion, but their article is an interesting one and helps highlight the complexity of this dilemma for narrative practitioners.

Hayward (2013) has also thought and written a lot about this topic. Having reviewed many of the larger meta-research studies, he stressed that frequently too much weight is given to the perceived specific treatment approach when it comes to the issue of therapeutic change. Indeed, he argued that the findings from many studies, when put into context, often do not support the claims made regarding their efficacy. For example, within his teaching notes, he refers to Wampold (2000) who reviewed thousands of studies, noting that only fifteen reported an advantage for cognitive behavioural therapy when approximately three thousand showed no difference. More recently, in 2006, Wampold and Brown reported that in the largest ever study on depression that compared cognitive behavioural therapy, inter-personal therapy, anti-depressants, and placebos, no significant difference was found in outcomes between any of the treatments given.

Hayward reflected that the three most effective clinicians or prescribers within this study were seen to achieve better outcomes compared to the three poorest, irrespective of what it was that they were prescribing, which included placebos. Furthermore, the difference between effective clinicians did not appear to relate to their age, gender, professional discipline, theoretical orientation, training undertaken, or personal therapy but rather on six other factors, these being the encouragement of people to use their own skills, knowledges, ideas, and preferences;

the focus on developing an understanding relationship with a person; an emphasis on working to achieve change in the short term; constant reflection; and the development of skills through deliberate practice; as well as a focus on tracking progress. Thus, it was the non-model-specific factors that appeared the most salient predictors of efficacy, and it could be argued that many of those identified would fit with a narrative therapy approach.

Current research

It is fair to say that there is a dearth of "gold-standard" evidence (i.e., perceived rigorous and statistically robust studies) for the effectiveness of narrative therapy. But there is an extensive number of publications on using narrative ideas therapeutically with individuals, couples, families, and communities. There is also a growing base of "effectiveness" and "efficacy" studies more in keeping with the structuralist ideas discussed. Yet the wider debate of cultivating research methodology more congruent with the principles of narrative therapy remains. For further information on the issue of research, we would direct readers to the Dulwich Centre website (www.dulwich centre.com.au), which provides a comprehensive and recent list of papers reviewing and discussing research, through to individual examples of research studies. Below are some examples that highlight the range of people, problems, and settings with which these ideas have been used.

Besa (1994) used narrative therapy techniques with six families. These techniques included externalisation, relative influence questioning, identifying and bringing forth unique outcomes and re-descriptions, facilitating circulation of alternative stories, and assigning between-session tasks. Compared to baseline rates, five of the six families showed improvements in parent–child conflict, ranging from an eighty-eight per cent to a ninety-eight per cent decrease in conflict. Improvements occurred only when narrative therapy was applied and were not observed in its absence.

Vromans and Schweitzer (2010) found a clinically significant improvement in self-reported symptoms of depression following eight sessions of manualised narrative therapy. Erbes, Stillman, Wieling, Bera, and Leskela (2014), by comparison, undertook a pilot study investigating the use of narrative therapy with fourteen veterans experiencing difficulties in keeping with a post-traumatic stress diagnosis.

Measures of trauma were regularly completed and the researchers found, following eleven to twelve sessions of narrative therapy, that three veterans no longer met the criteria for post-traumatic stress. The remaining eleven had a clinically significant decrease in symptoms. The study also reported a low drop-out rate together with a high level of reported satisfaction.

Augusta-Scott (2006), in his work with men who had committed acts of violence against women, reported positive change in groups that helped create space for men to develop alternative identity stories about themselves. Rather than the therapist assuming responsibility to "police" men's behaviour, Augusta-Scott reflected that by enabling other aspects of living to be more richly described, "a man's possible preference for honest, respectful relationships" is invited. Such conversations can have the effect of "a man eventually taking responsibility to 'police' himself, holding himself accountable for the effects of his ideas, feelings and actions" (Augusta-Scott, 2006, p. 30).

Poole, Gardner, Flower, and Cooper (2009) used narrative ideas in group work with older adults managing distress and substance misuse issues. They felt that the development of "alternative and empowering life stories" helped to "keep the problem in its place" (Poole, Gardner, Flower, & Cooper, 2009, p. 288). In 2006, Weber, Davis, and McPhie worked with seven women who self-identified as experiencing depression and problems with eating. The women participated in a group, informed by narrative therapy ideas, for ten weeks. Pre- and post-group measures were completed and a reduction found in "depression" scores and "eating disorder risk". The study also concluded that women reported a change in daily practice, and were engaged in less critical self-talk.

There can sometimes be an assumption that narrative therapy can only be used with people who have a strong command and understanding of language. However, research with children and young people suggests otherwise, as have studies looking at use of these ideas with individuals considered to have a learning disability. Stacey and Edwards (2013) found that a narrative therapy group intervention helped ameliorate the effects of loneliness in a group of men with learning disabilities. While McParland (2015) reviewed the use of narrative therapy with people with learning disabilities, and concluded overall tentative evidence of ameliorating difficulties, although the authors did go on to point out several methodological concerns with the reviewed studies' use of outcome measures, and problems with generalising the results due to the studies' designs.

Co-research

Co-research is a methodology that appears principally to have been coined and used within the narrative community (Epston, 1999; Epston & White, 1990), although its theoretical influences can be traced further back still (see Dulwich Centre Publications, 2004). Tootell (2004) reflected on trying to "find (or invent if necessary) a research approach that was consistent with [his] values and practice as a therapist" (Tootell, 2004, p. 54). He was particularly struck by the ideas of Michael White that therapy is "two-way", as this term helped ensure acknowledgement of the "contribution of the person, who has been consulting [the therapist], has made to the development of their skills and knowledge" (White, 1997, p. 130). Tootell felt the same principle applied to research, and that people should be considered "participants or co-researchers who act to influence or change the understandings of the principle researcher" (Tootell, 2004, p. 58).

Dulwich Centre Publications described how this "new form of ethnomethodology involve[s] inviting people of various cultures and communities to interpret and study their own lives and culture. In this way, the people and community being studied be[come] research partners and the research be[comes] accountable to local people" (2004, p. 30).

> I have always thought of myself as doing research, but on problems and the relationships people have with problems, rather than on people themselves. The structuring of narrative questions and interviews allows me and others to co-research problems and the alternative knowledges that are developed to address them.
>
> (Epston, 2001, p. 178)

Co-research appears, therefore, to offer an important alternative to the traditional forms of producing and circulating knowledge. It is a methodology consistent with narrative therapy ideas and focused on working with people, drawing on their knowledge about what *they* feel should be measured and important to change. It also actively resists dominant ideas that may objectify what research, or indeed therapy, should be about. For further information on co-research, we would encourage the reader to consult the Dulwich Centre website.

A final word

Our hope is that this book may be used as a scaffold for practitioners, and offer sufficient support to encourage the reader to practise narrative therapy. We hope that you enjoy it, and equally hope that you might share in the exciting and creative directions and possibilities that we have experienced in working with people using these ideas.

Acknowledgements

The editors would like to thank Hugh Fox and all members—past and present—of the Manchester Narrative Supervision Group.

References

Anderson, H. (2003). Postmodern social construction therapies. In: T. L. Sexton, G. R. Weeks, & M. S. Robbins (Eds.), *Handbook of Family Therapy: The Science and Practice of Working with Families and Couples* (pp. 125–146). New York: Routledge.

Augusta-Scott, T. (2006). Talking with men who have used violence in intimate relationships. *The International Journal of Narrative Therapy and Community Work, 4:* 23–30.

Beels, C. (2009). Some historical conditions of narrative work. *Family Process, 48:* 363–378.

Besa, D. (1994). Evaluating narrative family therapy using single-system research designs. *Research on Social Work Practice, 4:* 309–325.

Besley, A. C. (2002). Foucault and the turn to narrative therapy. *British Journal of Guidance and Counseling, 30:* 125–143.

Denborough, D. (2009). Reflecting on the legacies of Michael White. *Australian and New Zealand Journal of Family Therapy, 30:* 92–108.

Druker, A. (2014). What to do when a diagnosis doesn't fit. *The International Journal of Narrative Therapy and Community Work, 4:* 16–23.

Dulwich Centre Publications (2004). Narrative therapy and research. *The International Journal of Narrative Therapy and Community Work, 2:* 29–36.

Epston, D. (1999). Co-research: the making of alternative knowledge. In: *Narrative Therapy and Community Work: A Conference Collection.* Adelaide: Dulwich Centre Publications.

Epston, D. (2001). Anthropology, archives, co-research and narrative therapy. In: *Narrative Therapy and Community Work: A Conference Collection*. Adelaide: Dulwich Centre Publications.

Epston, D., & White, M. (1990). Consulting your consultants: the documentation of alternative knowledges. *Dulwich Centre Newsletter, 4*: 25–35.

Erbes, C. R., Stillman, J. R., Wieling, E., Bera, W., & Leskela, J. (2014). A pilot examination of the use of narrative therapy with individuals diagnosed with PTSD. *Journal of Traumatic Stress, 27*: 730–733.

Eysenck, H. J., & Eysenck, S. B. (1975). *Psychotism as a Dimension of Personality*. London: Hodder & Stoughton.

Foucault, M. (1980). Two lectures. In: C. Gordon (Ed.), *Power/Knowledge: Selected Interviews and Other Writings* (pp. 1972–1977). Hemel Hempstead: Harvester Wheatsheaf.

Fox, H. (2008). *Level 1 Narrative Training: A Four Day Course (Notes)*. Manchester: Centre for Narrative Practice.

Hayward, M. (2013). *Clinical Practice Intensive: Level 3 Module Notes*. London: The Institute of Narrative Therapy.

McParland, J. (2015). Narrative therapy in a learning disability context: a review. *Tizard Learning Disability Review, 20*: 121–129.

Poole, J., Gardner, P., Flower, M., & Cooper, C. (2009). Narrative therapy, older adults, and group work: practice, research, and recommendations. *Social Work with Groups, 32*: 288–302.

Stacey, J., & Edwards, A. (2013). Resisting loneliness' dark pit: a narrative therapy approach. *Tizard Learning Disability Review, 18*: 20–27.

Strong, T. (2012). Talking about the DSM-V. *The International Journal of Narrative Therapy and Community Work, 2*: 54–63.

Tootell, A. (2004). Decentring research practice. *The International Journal of Narrative Therapy and Community Work, 3*: 54–60.

Vromans, L. P., & Schweitzer, R. D. (2010). Narrative therapy for adults with major depressive disorder: improved symptom and interpersonal outcomes. *Psychotherapy Research, 19*: 4–15.

Vygotsky, L. (1986). *Thought and Language*. Cambridge, MA: MIT Press.

Wampold, B. E. (2001). *The Great Psychotherapy Debate: Models, Methods, and Findings*. Mahwah, NJ: Lawrence Erlbaum Associates.

Wampold, B. E., & Brown, J. (2006). Estimating variability in outcomes attributable to therapists: a naturalistic study of outcomes in managed care. *Journal of Consulting and Clinical Psychology, 73*: 914–925.

Weatherhead, S., & Jones, G. (2008). Measuring the narrative: the challenge of evidencing change in narrative therapy. *Clinical Psychology Forum, 188*: 38–41.

Weber, M., Davis, K., & McPhie, L. (2006). Narrative therapy, eating disorders, and groups: enhancing outcomes in rural New South Wales. *Australian Social Work, 59*: 391–405.

White, M. (1997). *Narratives of Therapists' Lives.* Adelaide: Dulwich Centre Publications.

White, M. (2004). Folk psychology and narrative practice. In: M. White (Ed.), *Narrative Practice and Exotic Lives: Resurrecting Diversity in Everyday Life* (pp. 59–118). Adelaide: Dulwich Centre Publications.

White, M. (2005). Workshop Notes. http://dulwichcentre.com.au/wpcontent/uploads/2014/01/michael-white-workshop-notes.pdf (accessed 21 September 2016).

White, M. (2007). *Maps of Narrative Practice.* New York: W. W. Norton.

CHAPTER ONE

Problem exploration

Lincoln Simmonds

Problem exploration in narrative therapy is not simply narrative therapy's equivalent to assessment. There is overlap with other therapeutic approaches in terms of the therapist exploring the quality of difficulties, the history of the concerns, and how the person is affected. However, the narrative therapist is not working to see how the person's difficulties fit with models or theories of mental health. Rather, problem exploration is a re-orientating of the person (and the therapist) in terms of how they view the problem. In narrative therapy, the purpose of problem exploration is to work towards an appreciation of the *person's* understanding of the problem. As with other therapies, the principles and assumptions of narrative therapy inform the assessment methods. Therefore, this chapter will begin by looking at these assumptions and principles, and how they inform practice.

I view problem exploration in narrative therapy as a foundation to re-authoring conversations. As the reader is aware, re-authoring conversations involve developing preferred stories. A preferred story is one that speaks of how the person wishes to live their life, in a way that is consistent with what they give value to. In order for a person to move towards preferred (or alternative) story development, the therapist helps the person examine and deconstruct the problem story that they bring to therapy, and this process will be discussed in this chapter.

Dominant discourses of how people experience difficulties can be very influential and often determine how people are viewed, and how people themselves relate to their own experiences. Such discourses exist in a framework of knowledge that states how these difficulties can or should be managed. People coming to therapy often have dominant (problem) stories about the difficulties they experience, which fit with dominant psychiatric, societal, or psychological models of mental health and wellbeing. These discourses of mental health are prominent, widely distributed, and strongly postulated within our society. However, such dominant problem stories may or *may not* be useful and helpful to the person. Problem exploration is about evaluating such discourses and their personal effects upon the person; as a potential entry point to an alternative story that fits better for the person. It is important to stress that this "storying" of the person's life is "authored" and "edited" by the person we are working with, not by the therapist. And that this storying may differ to a societal view of "how they should be".

Narrative, story

People come to therapy with some sense, some explanation, some story of how they are experiencing living with an illness. This story can come from many sources, such as the media, friends, family, and personal experiences. These stories or narratives are the central working material of narrative therapy. A narrative therapist seeks to explore and understand how the person sees the problem. This position requires the narrative therapist to explicitly acknowledge the expertise of the person as applied to his or her own experience.

Narrative therapy is also particularly careful to privilege the person's expertise before that of the therapist. Of course, the narrative therapist can share the knowledge and experience that they have, but this is offered to the person as one possibility among others, with the expectation that the person may or may not see these offerings as either useful or helpful ways of describing their personal experience. Hence the assumption is that the person is helped by the therapist to develop the story that fits best for them.

In a relationship with the problem

Narrative therapy seeks to help the person look at the problem as being separate to themselves. This is counter to ideas or stories that infer, or directly state, that problems relating to human experience are primarily intrinsic to the person. For example, a story that suggests some intrinsic deficit, failure, or weakness in a person might be one of:

> She has just not accepted that she has diabetes, after a while people have just got to "get on with it", but she keeps acting as if she doesn't want it.

The narrative therapist would instead invite the person to view themselves as being in a relationship with the problem:

> So how does The Diabetes affect you?
> Are there times when you just have enough of The Diabetes, and don't want anything to do with it at all?

The narrative therapist deliberately talks about the problem in relational terms: promoting (or rather offering) the idea that the problem and the person are in a relationship. This helps the person view the problem as being separate to their identity. The person may then begin to see the problem as acting on them, with the potential to then see how *they* can act upon the problem. The person and the problem are therefore seen as being in a mutual relationship, and having mutual influence upon each other.

Stories told, stories lived

Michael White (2005) emphasised that stories are not simply redundant descriptions of people's lived experiences. Stories actually have very real effects in that people can live by them. Stories circulated (about a person) can influence perceptions of other people, and thus how those people respond to the person. Difficulties can arise when stories we wish to hold about ourselves are in conflict with experiences. People who value stories of their independence, perhaps in terms of physical ability, may feel that a health condition instead means that they are reliant on others for care. Distress and difficulties can then ensue as a result of such views. Often, though, stories of a person giving value to independence may be less visible to healthcare staff than ones of a difficult and demanding "patient" or a person who seems to have "given up" and is not making progress.

A story circulated about a person having "given up" might lead professionals down a path of referring someone for psychological or psychiatric treatment, perhaps for depression. Whereas a less visible story about a person who feels that they have lost control over their lives could perhaps lead the team to respond to that person differently. Possibly in ways that could be more consistent with how the person wishes the team to work with them. These ideas remind the narrative therapist about the importance of developing stories that the person feels is most helpful to them. This would be in contrast to assuming that the most dominant story shared about a person is the starting point of intervention for us as therapists.

Deconstruction and contextualising

Narrative therapy seeks to deconstruct and contextualise a problem; or rather, the story about the problem (problem story). It endeavours to render the historical, social, relational, and cultural context within which a problem has developed to become known to the person.

She has just not accepted that she has diabetes.

The problem story illustrated implies that the "solution" to the problem is one of the person working to accept the diagnosis, and implications, of diabetes. This may be a helpful and useful storying for some people, in that they may be able to use this to make changes that they would regard as positive. However, it is often difficult to ascertain what such generalised statements mean. Is it a useful, accurate, and helpful story for that person? Does it really explain the particulars of this person's experience of living with diabetes?

The narrative therapist needs to understand specifically *that* person's experience, in order to learn (with the person) how best to help them. Such generalised problem stories often leave the worker with little sense of what the actual person thinks and feels, nor how the person acts in relation to the problem. Narrative therapy refers to such stories as "thin" descriptions of the problem. Thin because a more general view is far more likely to be a less detailed, assumptive description of a person's experience. Thin descriptions, however, are dominant in society:

> Well people tend to come to hospital feeling very unwell. We get them straight again with insulin, and they feel a lot better—relieved, in fact. Then as the days and weeks pass, and they realise that they have to keep testing their bloods. They learn that they have to look carefully at what they eat, and inject insulin. Well, that's when the problems start. It's at that point that they really just need to start accepting diabetes, and getting on with things.

The narrative therapist seeks to develop stories specific or more particular to the person's experience of their illness. In narrative therapy, these are called "experience near" descriptions. In the above example, the worker would explore how the problem of The Diabetes affects the person across situations, relationships, and time. The worker would be developing a thick (richer) description of the problem story. The example below highlights the differences between thin and thick descriptions:

A thin description

James and his family don't listen to the advice, I don't think they understand that he has a lifelong condition, and they can't just rely on exercise. He's just not accepting that he has diabetes. They've been lucky during the "honeymoon period", because the insulin has helped his pancreas whilst it is still working, but that won't last ...

A richer (thick) description of being in a relationship with diabetes

James' father and mother were both very fit people. His father did marathons and his mother was a wild swimmer. He had been training to compete for the district trials in the 400 m and 200 m, when Diabetes came into his life. It was hard for him to believe that he had diabetes: his family had always eaten healthily, no one else in his family had this diagnosis, and his parents had been very careful with his training regime. And yet The Diabetes seemed to have the control now. He wasn't sure he could rely on his body, or trust it any more. Mistrust and Feeling All at Sea seemed to be in league with The Diabetes. All he knew was to try and power through it, to make his body stronger, gain more control over it. He questioned how

> much insulin he should take: "Would his body become more and more reliant on it?"; "Might his diabetes get worse?"; perhaps there were other ways, other more natural approaches? Couldn't he control his blood sugar through just being very fit and eating well?

Multi-storied lives

Dominant stories are often put forward as right, correct, or true explanations of human experience. This practice is supported by the idea that knowledge can be derived generally from people's experiences, and then accurately applied to an individual's unique experience. Thus, it can be argued from this position that each person's experience of living can be reduced to general explanatory categories and statements.

> People with cancer often go through the stages of loss: shock/denial; anger; depression; bargaining; and acceptance upon hearing about their diagnosis.

Narrative therapy would rather argue that there are many ways of viewing an illness, and many stories of how people experience it. If a worker enters conversations with people from such a position, then they are more likely to co-develop stories with people. Stories that from the person's viewpoint fit best with their lived experience.

> Yes, you're right, I have seen many people who have had to live with cancer and they have taught me many things. I have learned that people can respond to this diagnosis in different ways, and there are many ideas around about how people respond. But can you tell me how The Diagnosis is affecting you?

Working with skills and knowledges

Problem exploration is essentially about creating a foundation to support the development of preferred alternative stories for a person. Problem exploration helps provide a multitude of entry points to developing less visible and preferred (by the person) stories. Discussions about skills and knowledges are about the development of entry points. Michael White (2007) often talked about the importance of exploring skills and knowledges of a person prior to problem exploration. He felt that such exploration provided "a platform" from which a person can explore the difficulties. Hence serving as a base from which a person can explore the problem without feeling overwhelmed by it, as the person is more aware of aspects of life separate to the problem. The person may also potentially see ways of using their skills and knowledges to act upon the problem and ameliorate its effects.

Exploration of skills and knowledges also serves as a reminder to us that narrative therapy is not a serial or linear therapy. It is rather the development of a constellation of relations and understandings.

Leslie, you've told me how The Crohn's Disease saps your energy. I'm wondering about your Creativity and Knowledge of Art History ... are they ever affected by The Crohn's Disease?

Are there times when your energy is replenished or drains less slowly when you step into Being Creative? Does low energy sometimes mean that you lose touch with your interest in Art History?

Externalising conversations

You may have noted that in this chapter capital letters have been used to describe a problem or a skill or knowledge in the case examples. This is known as naming and is part of a practice called externalising. Externalising conversations were first developed and written about by Michael White (1984). White observed that people would often come into therapy sessions with an "internalised" understanding of the problem. For example, "I am bad" or "my child is naughty". In this way, the problem had very much become part of the person's identity. It was noted that these internalised understandings not only had the effect of rendering a person powerless to do anything about the problem, but could also exacerbate the problem yet further.

The broad aims of externalising conversations are to move away from this internalised understanding to a position where the *problem is separate from the person*. From this externalised position, distance can be created between the person and the problem. The person can be viewed as separate to the problem, but in a relationship with the problem. In creating this distance, White (2007) believed that it allowed new understandings of the problem to develop. People are better able to see how the problem affects them, but crucially may then be able to explore how they can affect the problem; thus opening possibilities that the person has some agency or power in being able to ameliorate, or diminish, the effects of a problem on their life.

> Maggie spoke of how being a woman living with a bowel disease meant that she couldn't go out as often as she wanted to, as she was frequently too ill to leave the house. However, when asked how the bowel disease affected her, she talked about IT (the bowel disease) undermining her confidence to take on new activities or responsibilities. She also said that the bowel disease had her doing a lot of planning and accounting for nearby toilets, or thinking carefully about timings around when she last had a meal in order to manage any trips out.

It can be useful to develop a name for the problem; doing so can support the separation of the person from the problem as well as help personify the problem. Separation of the person from the problem can assist a person with the process of taking a position on the problem. By giving the problem a name, the worker can start to impose a chosen identification of the problem, thus imparting some control over it (Payne, 2006). Personification can also allow exploration of actions and tactics that the problem can elicit, and so begin to open up conversations around how a person responds.

Naming develops a shared language from which to talk about the problem, again allowing new understandings to develop, and often reducing the blame felt by the use of more structural/internalised language. Through this shared use of language, we can move away from family members or medical teams "versus" the person, towards uniting in the shared endeavour of understanding the problem and finding ways to cope with it.

It is important that the person seeking therapy is the one who decides what should be named and what that name is. If people struggle with naming, then the worker can offer a name for the problem. This would only be done under the explicit condition that if people think of a name that fits better for them, then the worker would substitute the previous name for that. Often drawing on names that other people have used (who have experienced similar difficulties with illness) can be helpful in facilitating naming. Identifying a name that is distinct from a formal diagnostic or medical label creates movement towards an experience-near (or thick) description of the problem.

> Maggie was all too happy to ditch the medical name for her condition, and instead frequently talked about her physical symptoms primarily in terms of The Bubbling. By this, she not only referred to the feelings in her bowels that warned of a possible need to go to toilet, but also to a bubbling of emotions such as The Worry, or The Frustration, or The Hopelessness.

Alongside naming the problem, and at times instead of using words, many people find it helpful to characterise the problem by visually representing it in a drawing or diagram. People can often use objects to represent the problem, or may wish to create the problem out of clay, Lego, or Plasticine. This gives the added dimension of being able to change or modify the model as new ideas or understandings develop.

> A colleague spoke of using Play-Doh with young people, and added how the young people would begin to reduce the size of the model of the problem over time, as they learned new ways of managing the problem and reducing its presence in their lives.

The principles of externalisation are relatively straightforward; however, in practice, it can take time to use externalising conversations in a creative and individual way. Russell and Carey (2003) described externalisation not simply as a technique or skill, but as an attitude and orientation in conversations. In order to have externalising conversations, it is essential to have some understanding of the theoretical basis on which narrative therapy stands.

When thinking about how to approach using externalising conversations, it can be useful to think about Michael White's metaphor of a therapist as an "investigator reporter". This position is far removed from the "expert" health professional role that may be familiar to most people, and instead places the therapist in a position of the "curious investigator" who needs information in order to understand the problem. The person seeking support then moves into a position of "informant" with insider knowledge on the problem.

The investigator reporter position also highlights that, although a therapist may not be neutral (i.e., the therapist is not on the problem's side!), it is important that the therapist does not jump to conclusions or make assumptions. White (2007) considers this stance to be particularly important in that it helps avoid taking a "totalising" position on the problem, in which a problem is considered all good or all bad. For example, if we were to assume that a person wanted to rid themselves of Worry in relation to their diabetes, we may ignore the value that a person places on some aspects of Worry, such as the belief that Worry helps to ensure adherence to the dietary requirements of diabetes.

Within any time-measured system (including the NHS), there may be pressures to jump to conclusions about the nature of the problem. In doing so, we risk externalising a problem based upon our understandings and not the person's. Michael White, within workshops, would often talk about "loitering", which we interpret as spending time with a problem: exploring it in order to begin to see potential options for externalising with the person. This is in contrast to being too quick to externalise what the therapist feels is "helpful". We highlight this by returning to the previous story about Maggie and her bowel condition:

> So Maggie, you've talked about all The Planning involved with going out, and The Concern whether you will have an accident whilst you're away from home. You also told me about The Reluctance to make the effort at all: what do you think is most important for us to talk about at the moment?

Hence the worker loiters over potential options to develop externalising conversations, and of course offer options to the person as to what fits best for them. It is also important from the outset to use the person's own language. This helps ensure that the descriptions elicited belong to the person, and are not provided to them by the therapist.

Within our exploration, we are also likely to identify a number of problems. The worker will not only negotiate the focus of the conversation with the person, but also which problem to focus on at any one time. The narrative therapist would also be interested in exploring the potential relationships between problems. Thus, returning to the example of Maggie talking about her bowel problem:

> Maggie, I'm just wondering does The Concern lead to more of The Planning? Do The Reluctance and The Concern work together to prevent you from leaving the house?

Within our culture, we are accustomed to internalised understanding of problems. People will often talk about willpower and inner strength in terms of their "fight" with an illness. There is a sense that some people are simply "very strong", and that they have particular aspects of their fixed personality that enable them to manage difficulties well. We often see such themes repeated again and again within the media. These themes seem to fit with ideas inherent in Westernised society of the individual asserting themselves, and drawing on fixed personality characteristics, in order to overcome adversity and "succeed" in life. So, for many people, externalising conversations can represent a very different type of conversation. It is a type of conversation that suggests that how we respond to the adversities and challenges of illness might be more helpfully conceptualised as contextual and relational.

> What makes it easier for you to go to work, and what makes it harder?
> Who supports you in getting to work?
> Are there times when The Fatigue wins?
> How does it manage to come out on top sometimes?

It can be useful to regularly "check in" with a person throughout all of externalising conversations and ask:

> Am I getting/hearing this right?
> Does this fit with your understanding?
> Is there something that we have missed, or that feels more important to talk about?

Thus, within externalising conversations, the worker seeks to move away from expressions that imply that the person's character and attributes are "fixed", to ones that view them as contextual. The worker thinks about the person having skills and knowledges that can be supported and tapped into more easily depending upon the context. Shifting the adjectives that people can use to describe themselves, for example Weak or Useless, into nouns (or perhaps pronouns) such as The Weakness, can facilitate this process. The therapist can use the gerund of verbs (i.e., the present continuous of verbs, usually with "ing" on the end; e.g., moving, taking, pursuing) to give more of a sense of problems shifting over time and context. The worker may talk about "feeling" Weakness, "using" Strength to thus orientate the person away from fixed internal descriptions of themselves, and towards their relationship with particular problems or desired skills or knowledges.

There is an assumption in narrative therapy that a problem's relationship with a person will fluctuate over time. Through such exploration, we can begin to understand more about what potentially exacerbates (as well as ameliorates) a problem's hold over a person, over time. Thus the therapist will tend to use questions that help with exploration of the entire history of a problem's presence within a person's life. For example:

> Maggie when did The Reluctance first start to show its face in your life?
> Are there times when The Concern is around more? Or less?
> What do you feel sustains The Reluctance?
> When was The Reluctance at its strongest?

Questions such as these help begin to place the problem into a storyline; it can also be useful to use "relative influence questioning" (White & Epston, 1990, p. 42). These types of questions invite people to talk about the effects of the problem on their life, but also crucially the influence of their experience, actions, and relationships on the problem. Such questions can be revelatory to people, in terms of them realising that they can actually have an effect on the problem, as opposed as to the problem solely acting on them:

> Maggie, are there times when you are able to push The Reluctance to the back of your mind, and still see your friends?

It is also helpful and important to externalise strengths (narrative therapists prefer the term "qualities"). As noted above, recognition of skills and knowledge are important in supporting people not to feel overwhelmed by problems. Through the process of creating distance between the person within externalising conversations, we can uncloak or unmask previously hidden choices and actions taken, skills and understandings. Through the externalisation of perceived strengths, we make them more visible and available to a person. These qualities can then be accessed and marshalled in managing the effects of the dominant problem:

> Maggie, how do you do that?
> How are you able to go out despite The Reluctance?
> Are there particular things that you know that help you do that?
> What do you draw on in being able to get out of the door?
> How do your skills in Planning help with being able to meet your friends at the cafe?

SOPM1/externalising conversations map

Maps in narrative therapy are essentially pathways, or sequences of questions, that aim to assist and guide the therapist into a particular conversational area. White (2007) described the aim of these maps as increasing the transparency of, and ability to replicate, the practice. All maps are intended as guidelines only: they are in no way meant to be prescriptive and require personalising for each individual.

Statement of Position Map One (SOPM1), also sometimes referred to as the "Externalising Conversations Map", aims to explore the problem that has been brought to therapy. White suggests that this map can be particularly helpful when people attend with a problem-saturated account of their lives, and/or when they have negative conclusions about their identity (White, 2007). Haywood (2013) also highlighted that the map is particularly helpful when you feel that a problem needs acknowledgement. SOPM1 is often used at the start of therapy. However, it can also be utilised when a new problem arises, or to check the continued helpfulness of the developed description for a person as understandings develop.

Narrative therapy does not solely focus on the problem that is brought to therapy; however, exploring the problem remains an important aspect of the therapeutic process. SOMP1 extends on externalising practice and supports the separation of the person from the problem. SOPM1 is referred to as a *position map* because it focuses on the exploration of what is important to the person seeking therapy. Through this process, it assists them to develop their own position on the problem, that is, what is helpful/not helpful about it. White (2007) highlights that through this map the therapist's position is more clearly defined within the "decentred but influential" role, which encourages a collaborative working relationship to develop.

SOMP1 is made up of four lines of enquiry, and is represented in the grid below:

1. Naming the problem	2. Exploring the effects
3. Evaluation of the effects	4. Justification

Figure 1.1. The four areas of enquiry in SOP1.

The first box of the grid relates to the development of a name or definition of the problem (naming the problem; one). Following this, the map moves onto considering and mapping the effects of the problem (exploring the effects; two). The third stage supports the evaluation of the effects identified in stage two (evaluation; three), and the final stage relates to identifying how the evaluated effects relate to what is important to the person; thus what they give value to in their lives, and to what extent the problem and its effects fit with what they want for their life (justification; four). As with all the maps in narrative therapy, the therapist is not required to work through these stages in order and can move between lines of enquiry, as it is felt necessary.

Enquiry area one aims to assist people to define the problem, or problems, for which they have attended therapy. As discussed, it is important that that this definition or name reflects the understanding of the person seeking therapy, not an experience-distant definition such as "non-adherence to medication" or "health anxiety".

In response to the problem being defined as "health anxiety", it can be useful to characterise the "health anxiety" in terms of how the person particularly experiences this in their lives:

What does The Health Anxiety have you doing? How does it affect how you feel about yourself? What feelings does it evoke when present? What does it persuade you to think during these times?

Through unpacking initial descriptions of problems in this way, we move from a general (perhaps textbook) experience-distant description of the problem, to a more personalised (experience-near) description that is unique to that individual. During the course of such characterisation, the person may rename the problem to something more unique to their experience. For example, the previous description of health anxiety might be renamed The Wave of Uncertainty.

The second stage draws out the influence or effects of the problem. The effect of the problem can be far-reaching. It can be useful to explore the impact, not only on the person, their relationships, their work or school, and mood, but also on how the person views themselves and the world. We do not need to achieve a comprehensive list of the effects, rather a good understanding of the principle effects.

For example, exploring how "The Wave of Uncertainty" has impacted upon a person's life:
Has The Wave of Uncertainty ever impacted upon your enjoyment of going out to meet friends?
Does The Wave of Uncertainty ever turn up at your work?'
What does The Wave of Uncertainty have you thinking about yourself?
Do you have any sense of what The Wave of Uncertainly wants for your life?
Does it any way try to dictate how you should live your life?

The third stage seeks to look further at the effects of the problem, in order to support people to take a position on the problem. It can be helpful for the therapist to recap and summarise everything discussed ("editoralise") at this stage. During this exploration, the person can state which aspects of the problem are wanted by them, and which are not. For example, there may be elements of The Wave of Uncertainty that a person finds helpful, and others aspects that they feel are less tolerable.

Are you in favour of it?
Whose interests do you feel The Wave of Uncertainty has at heart?
Are there any parts of The Wave of Uncertainty that feel helpful for you?
What has been good or not so good about having The Wave of Uncertainty present in your life?

The fourth area of enquiry looks at these positions taken by the person in relation to the problem(s), and asks *why* they have come to these conclusions.

Why is it not OK with you that The Wave of Uncertainty stops you from leaving the house?
Why is it important to you that you are able to leave the house when you choose?
What is not leaving the house stopping you from achieving?
Why is it helpful for you that The Wave of Uncertainty can act as a signal to take more care?
Why does checking your body, an action encouraged when The Wave of Uncertainty is around, feel important to you?

Through this line of questioning, it is hoped that we can explore and verbalise people's values, their aspirations and commitments. It can also open the door to contradictions to the negative conclusions or dominant narratives that people have drawn. During the course of using SOPM1, it is very likely that the therapist will have developed multiple lines of inquiry with the person. There may be a number of effects (of the problem) described, which may each have *both* positive and negative evaluations. Through this process, a number of values (justifications) may also be identified, and used to support a person to decide how they wish to position themselves in relation to the problem. The simplest way to discern the course to take through the conversation is by simply asking the person their preference. This transcript with Maggie helps highlight the multiplicity of possibilities that externalising conversations can develop:

THERAPIST:	So you talked about how The Bubbles often lead to there being more Reluctance to go out, and that often The Reluctance is driven by The Concern (The Therapist seeks to clarify that the named problem leads to effects of The Reluctance, which link to The Concern)
MAGGIE:	Erm ... yes
THERAPIST:	How would you view The Concern? Would it be something that you want in your life? (An evaluation question about The Concern)
MAGGIE:	I'm not sure ... sometimes it can be helpful, you know it sort of means that I take care when I go out, make sure that there are toilets around and that I don't stay out too long. Other times, though, it just almost makes me freeze, and well ... . I guess my friends are used to me phoning them at the last minute to cancel ... but then I feel bad, guilty, and like I've missed out (Maggie answers by voicing both positive and negative effects of The Concern)
THERAPIST:	So sometimes The Concern can stop you going out with friends, and can lead to Guilt coming round? (Asking about how The Guilt and The Concern relate to one another)
MAGGIE:	And guilt makes me even more reluctant to make plans the next time.
THERAPIST:	It sounds like The Reluctance stopping you from going out really isn't something that you want, is that right? [Maggie nods] So

> could you tell me why going out with friends is so important to you? (The therapist seeks an evaluation of The Reluctance, and then asks further questions to help explore what Maggie is giving value to by continuing to want to go out with her friends.)

Further examples of questions that can be used within each category of the SOPM1 (White, 2005) include:

Naming questions:	Effects questions:
• If you could see the problem, what would it look like?	• How long has this problem been in your life?
• How does it make you feel when it is around?	• What does it have you thinking about yourself?
• Would it have a voice?	• How do you know when it is around?
• Would you be able to draw it or shape it out of these materials?	• Are there times when the influence of the problem is really strong?
• Having talked about these difficulties, I am wondering if any particular images come to mind?	• Are there times when it is easier to forget about the problem, or carry on despite it being around?
• What name would you give to this problem?	• How does the problem affect your work or schooling?
• I could suggest a name that other people have used for these difficulties … would you like me to do that … how does that name fit with your experience?	• What sorts of effects does the problem have on your friendships? Or relationships with family? Or the medical team?
	• Was there ever a time when you were free of this problem? Or when it was less of a problem for you?
	• What does this problem have you thinking about your life and your hopes for the future?
	• Is there anything that's helpful about having this problem around? Is there anything that it makes you pay more attention to that feels useful, or has it led you to particular understandings of the world that you value?

Evaluation questions:	Justification questions:
• Is this okay with you? • How do you feel about this? • How is this by you? • Where do you stand on this/ where would you like to stand? • What is your position on this? • Is this a positive or negative development in your life? • Or would you say both a positive and a negative development, or neither of these? • Or would you say an in-between development?	• Why is/isn't this okay for you? • Why do you feel this way about this development? • How come you're taking this stand/ position on this development? • Would you tell me a story about your life that would help me to understand why you would take this position on this development? • What does taking this position on this, in this way, tell you/me about what you consider important, or your hopes for your life?

In conclusion

By now, the reader will have a broader understanding of how problem exploration is not a process of assessing people by eliciting information, to refer to, in terms of prescribed categories of emotional well-being. Problem exploration is in itself a narrative therapy orientation. Problem-exploring conversations are a first step towards scaffolding preferred stories. Frequently, a person may struggle to know why a particular problem is bothering them. Having space to become clearer about what it is, and how precisely it is affecting them, is important. As once a problem is "mapped out", it is usually easier for a person to tell a therapist what they think about aspects of the problem. It also becomes easier for a person to think about how they would like their life to be (frequently, if asked this straight away, it is too big a question). Both the therapist and person can then work to identify those times that do not fit with the problem story and to begin to story these. Furthermore, returning to problem-exploration conversations at various stages in the therapeutic journey can be useful, as problem accounts tend to evolve over time, and as a person becomes clearer about what it is that the problem actually refers to.

Acknowledgements

With many thanks to Hannah Fielden for coming along on the ride. Your fresh pair of eyes and comments were invaluable to me in writing this chapter. And of course to D, I, & R. LS.

References

Haywood, M. (2013). *Externalising Practice: Statement of Position Map 1.* Adelaide: Dulwich Centre Publications.

Payne, M. (2006). *Narrative Therapy* (2nd edn.). London: Sage.

Russell, S., & Carey, M. (2003). Outsider-witness practices: some answers to commonly asked questions. *International Journal of Narrative Therapy and Community Work, 1*: 3–16. [Republished in: S. Russell & M. Carey (Eds.), *Narrative Therapy: Responding to Your Questions* (pp. 63–90). Adelaide: Dulwich Centre Publications, 2004.]

White, M. (1984). Pseudo-encopresis: from avalanche to victory, from vicious to virtuous cycles. *Family Systems Medicine, 2*: 150–160.

White, M. (2005). Workshop notes. http://dulwichcentre.com.au/wp-content/uploads/2014/01/michael-white-workshop-notes.pdf (accessed 17 November).

White, M. (2007). *Maps of Narrative Practice.* New York: W. W. Norton.

White, M., & Epston, D. (1990). *Narrative Means to Therapeutic Ends.* New York: W. W. Norton.

CHAPTER TWO

Re-authoring conversations

Louise Mozo-Dutton and Rachel Skippon

People come to therapy with stories about themselves that are in some way interfering with the lives they would prefer to lead. Yet problematic stories will only ever be one version of lived experience, a partial description of a person's identity and the events within their lives. Re-authoring is the process by which people are supported to develop alternative accounts of themselves: accounts that they prefer. The therapist does this by listening out for those hopeful moments that may have become neglected or overshadowed by the problem story. Narrative theory suggests that these moments can be richly described; the richer their description, the greater their possibility for influence (White, 2007). This being so, as stories become more vivid and visible to a person, they also become easier to access and metaphorically step into. Thus in order to thicken a developing story, meaning is deepened and moments connected to others within a person's history. Encouraging a re-engagement with stories that have been hidden from view offers the possibility for the resurrection of alternative knowledge, skills, values, hopes, and dreams. This can lead to the development of new (or even old) understandings that fit better with the way a person would like to see themselves, be seen by others, or go on in life.

In this chapter, we (Rachel and Louise) intend to outline a number of steps that may be used to support and scaffold re-authoring conversations, with one therapeutic example referred to throughout to help illustrate the "how to" at each stage.

But first a note: multi-storied lives

The practice of re-authoring can often be subject to the misconception that there is one problem story to which only one alternative story should be developed as a counter; this is an idea that tends to pitch one description against another. Yet single-storied accounts appear more in keeping with structuralist ideas, which promote a view of self that is largely fixed and unchanging throughout life. The privileging of just one account, therefore, and even if preferred, may still serve to reduce or restrain a person in some way. White and Epston (1990) instead propose that people are multi-storied, and that multiple accounts offer more opportunities for living and seeing ourselves. Thus in order to avoid closing down possibilities, a therapist is encouraged to focus on the development of multiple alternatives. Co-constructed stories do not necessarily have to be consistent with one another, or even clear and coherent: as our intentions and actions will at times appear contradictory, and it is important that our stories reflect this. A multi-storied approach recognises that there is space for stories that conflict to co-exist.

Step one: exploring the many contexts of a person's life

Stories referred to as "dominant" tend to loom large within therapeutic conversations. They frequently direct their flow and content, and can make it difficult for a therapist to circumvent and hear about other aspects of a person's life. This is especially so for people living with a physical health problem, where the condition has the potential to limit life or markedly affect function. Yet as dominant stories may never fully encompass all within their description, it is always possible to begin dismantling their influence and to start forging pathways around or even through the problem.

The first step in this process is to learn as much as possible about a person and their lived experience. At this point, a therapist does not need to do anything, just simply get these stories out there and listen carefully. This practice is also considered to support the ongoing separation of the problem from the person, in that "Sarah" becomes less likely to be seen as "Sarah with breast cancer", or Tom as "Tom the diabetic". Encouraging conversations that are rich in detail also make it more likely that exceptions to a problem story will begin to come to the fore. We would now like to introduce you to Suzanne.

Suzanne lives with her partner Dave, and her two daughters Emma (aged seven) and Jessica (aged nine). Suzanne's parents both died when she was in her teens: she was therefore brought up by her older sister and grandmother, who had since passed away. Eighteen years ago, when Suzanne was in her early twenties, she had an accident at work carrying heavy boxes. She injured her back and has struggled with back pain ever since.

Suzanne had been repeatedly referred into the chronic pain team. She had undergone many different medical interventions over the years, all of which had been largely unsuccessful in reducing her pain. In referral meetings, the team would reflect on Suzanne's apparent "disengagement". For instance, she was reported to have not arrived for appointments with the team physiotherapists and nurses, and to have repeatedly sought higher levels of medication. Her presentation was viewed by some as "functional" in that they believed it served some intentional purpose. The team were aware of some of the other troubles that Suzanne was facing in her life, including financial stress and a difficult relationship with her sister.

Suzanne was referred for "psycho-social" support to enable her to "accept" and make lifestyle choices to facilitate living more tolerably with her chronic pain. In our first meeting, Suzanne explained:

"It's my back. I'm in pain all the time. It makes me tired and irritable. I don't have the energy for all the things I need to do, let alone want to do. I'm useless. I'm weak and don't put enough effort into getting on with life. It's been like this for so long now. Ever since the accident at work, I've never been able to achieve anything; I'm good for nothing. The doctors aren't interested in me, they say there's nothing else they can do for me and I need to do more for myself, but I just can't. My sister agrees and tells me it's my fault because I'm weak and lazy. She's always telling me "when I was growing up, we didn't have time for whining, we just got on with it". I can't escape my pain and tiredness: it controls everything. I have no choice. I never know how the day is going to go. I'm sure I'll be sacked from my job soon; they are fed up of me taking too much time off. I get so worried thinking how we're going to manage without the money, we struggle enough as it is, and this makes everything worse because I get so worried. No matter what I do, it's never good enough and life just hurts."

Hearing Suzanne's words helps to highlight the level of influence that pain, and the stories told about pain, were having on her life. They had created a particular perspective, and in doing so were obscuring other possible views. Stories do not exist in isolation, and others were therefore involved in the creation and re-telling of stories about Suzanne. The team told a problem-saturated story where "all" of Suzanne's behaviour was viewed through a lens of "how a good patient should behave", and against this criterion she was judged to have "failed". Expectations of how a person "should be" were also perpetuated by those closest to Suzanne. The idea of just getting on with it may have worked for her sister, but for Suzanne this was simply used to further confirm her perceived failure as a person. There are many ways in which a therapist can begin to move onto conversations about life outside of a problem, but first let's return to Suzanne.

> Through conversation, Suzanne concluded that the biggest problem was not the pain itself but the control it had over her life. "It's just this thing that controls everything, I never know from one hour to the next what is going to happen, how I'm going to manage; it's like living under a really awful boss."
> Suzanne felt that a good name for the problem was "The Boss". This captured something of the way in which its control appeared to extend to almost every aspect of her life, the unpredictable experience of it, and the feeling she was left with, that she had no choice in what happened.
> Talking about The Boss enabled Suzanne and I to explore some of the effects the presence of The Boss was having on her life. These included:
> • Not feeling able to plan ahead. This created a lot of problems for Suzanne at work and in being there for her young children—coping with their day-to-day care.
> • Not feeling able to plan also had a significant impact on Suzanne's social life in that she barely went out any more and felt that she had lost closeness with almost all of her former friends.

- The difficulty Suzanne experienced in resisting The Boss's plans also provided "evidence" for Suzanne of her apparent incompetence in many areas of life. For example, those times where she would measure herself against ideas such as "getting on with it", "succeeding" at work, being a "good mum", and being a "strong person".

Some ideas to support alternative conversations

Genograms (McGoldrick, Gerson, & Shellenberger, 1999) have been used extensively within family therapy, and are a great way of exploring who or what may have contributed to a person and in what way. In addition to the traditional mapping of a person's family, a therapist might wish to draw out an "alternative" genogram whereby the focus is on *any* relationship considered special to a person. This could include people who have died, neighbours, teachers, work colleagues, friends, pets, objects, and books among others. In the current times, influences might include music groups or lyrics, particular podcasts, You Tube[rs], gamers, athletes, and celebrity figures. Enquiring as to their significance or contribution to a person's life can support exploration of important relationships further. This practice is known as re-membering (Russell & Carey, 2002; White, 2007).

Looking through photos also offers a unique opportunity to find out about significant relationships, as well as situations or stories with which a person may have lost touch. Responding to written text such as literature, emails, letters, phone messages or even cards sent, is another means by which this can be done. Simchon (2013) used poetry with women facing terminal cancer. Each week, group members were asked to read a poem: a conversation would then be facilitated based upon the words that were found to have resonated most. Though considered a "talking therapy", narrative conversations frequently draw on non-verbal information, which can be "storied" simply by enquiring as to its meaning or significance. Using genograms and photos are examples of this, but you might just as easily consider observations of play or other mediums such as painting, collecting special objects, clothes worn by a person, or hairstyles. Problematic accounts may also be traversed simply by asking what a person enjoys, with whom they value spending time, or what hopes they have for the future.

During our meetings, it became clear that Suzanne's children were a big part of her life. Suzanne would show me photographs of her daughters on her phone. Spending time looking at these pictures, and hearing the little stories behind each one, prompted and brought to life many ideas and reflections for Suzanne, not only of her hopes and dreams for her girls but also of her intentions as a Mum.

They opened up space for different kinds of talking outside of the problem-saturated story. Suzanne told me that this made her experience of coming to "pain team appointments" as she had come to know them, very different and "something to look forward to instead of dread, cos I know I'm not coming for a telling off of all the things I'm doing wrong".

Feeling more comfortable in sessions seemed to help Suzanne explore possibilities about her life and the way she would like to live it—feeling less constrained by what she had previously felt she "ought to be feeling, doing, or thinking".

Step two: careful listening

In this step, it is a therapist's job to jot down any possible "gaps" within the problem story. Thus, any small moments, responses, beliefs, feelings, or actions that do not seem to fit with the problem story or any other aspects of life and identity that appear important for a person. These seemingly small inconsistencies or points of interest are referred to as unique outcomes, exceptions, or sparkling moments. They might relate to a tangible event, achievement, or action or to a more abstract experience, for example, beliefs, hopes, or desires that a person had remained in touch with during a difficult time. When you hear an example of a unique outcome, encouraging a careful and experience-near description of the event is a good starting point (Winslade & Hedtke, 2008). However, it is also important that the therapist remains open to hearing about other (possible) unique outcomes, rather than immediately developing the first one shared, as this might mean missing others considered more important to a person later down the line. The therapist can simply note down each moment and return to explore their significance at another point.

Suzanne and an example of a unique outcome

R: Are there any times when you have thought or done something that doesn't go along with The Boss's plans for you? Any times when you've taken some control back?

S: Well, there was this time when both my girls had a day off school. I was determined to do something nice with them, but the pain was just awful when I woke, probably because I'd worked extra hours in the week so I could have the day off. I'd planned to go swimming but knew I couldn't face that. Anyway the girls were really good and just amused themselves in the morning while I lay on the sofa after I'd taken my tablets. Then later, we made rice crispie cakes at home. It didn't take much, but the girls really enjoyed it. I let them get messy and lick the bowl. It was a really nice time.

R: What was different about this time? What were you trying to do in putting in that effort to spend time making cakes with your daughters?

S: It felt like I was being a proper Mum. Like doing things with them, spending time with them … encouraging them. It was like we had a closer relationship somehow. I made time for them, and they knew they are important to me. So The Boss didn't stop me being there for them, and they knew that.

R: And why is that so important to you?

S: It's … having people, parents, around you who are there for you, who you know and they understand you and encourage you, that's really important to kids. It helps them to feel loved and they'll be confident adults. I want my kids to feel loved and that they're good enough, that they are important enough, that I will spend time with them.

R: Looking back on how that day panned out now, do you have any other thoughts about it?

S: Normally I might have thought it was another day when I let them down because really in terms of time, I couldn't manage much. We didn't go swimming like I'd hoped but talking like this has helped me realise that, although making the cakes only took about half an hour and the girls had spent most of the morning on their own, making the cakes with me is what they remembered about that day, and I know they really enjoyed it. So I'm not listening to the thoughts that I failed that day because I don't think I did.

Double listening and the absent but implicit (ABI)

White argued that a person can only understand what something is by knowing what it is not (Derrida, 1978; White, 2000). This practice is referred to as "double listening" and asks a person to listen to not only what is being said, but also to what is not, as well as consider what the being said might relate to. The latter of these points is known as the "absent but implicit" (White, 2000, 2005). Thus, it is "absent" in that it is not directly discussed, yet it is "implicit" in that it provides the background that enables understanding. For example, when a person talks about depressed mood, this will mean that they also have some knowledge of mood minus depression. For someone to talk about hopelessness or despair means that they will have had contact with hope or ideas about what a life with hope would look like. The presence of anger, by contrast, may relate to wider ideas about justice, fairness, or equality that have been shaken. In this vein, distress might be more usefully conceptualised as an ongoing tribute to precious values or aspirations that have been damaged in some way. They would be unlikely to cause upset if they no longer mattered to a person. The "problem", therefore, can be taken to signal that a person is not content with the *status quo* and instead wishes for something to be different in their life.

Suzanne and the ABI

s: I'm so sick of The Boss being in control the whole time. I can't cope with it any more.

r: What is it that you're refusing to go along with when you express this feeling?

s: The control it has over everything—my whole life. I just want to be able to be free of it. To decide what I'll do today rather than have it decided for me by The Boss.

r: It sounds like there's something important to you about control and freedom. Something that is precious to you that you are speaking up for?

s: Yes. I just can't go on like this. It's not fair; I deserve a better chance than this.

r: A chance for what?

s: To be a good Mum and partner, to be able to get on at work, and maybe get a better job one day so that we can manage money better.

To have a chance to look after myself a bit, to have a laugh and be one of the girls. Being able to be consistent and provide a stable time for my girls is really important. The Boss tries to take that away all the time.

R: By talking about how you feel about the difficulties The Boss can put in your path, do you think that you are going along with its plans or are you taking a different path?

S: I guess I'm fed up of it. I'm saying it's not alright.

R: Would you see that as some sort of protest?

S: I suppose so. I'm just not accepting it any more. Sometimes I think I don't care about the consequences; I'm going to do what I want to do, even though I know I'll probably pay for it later.

R: Have you ever tried it out? Doing what you want to do even though you think you might "pay for it later"? How did it go?

S: There was a time; it was a quite a while ago, when they were having a work night out. Usually I wouldn't dream of going, I really can't manage, so I wouldn't even try. I often feel a bit out of things because I never go on the nights out and because I've had quite a bit of time off, I feel like I don't get on as well with the other girls at work. They all seem to know each other really well. I start to think, "well, they probably don't want me there, just being boring, not drinking and going home early". But this time, Sharon, the girl next to me, said "Oh come on, you only live once, at least come for the meal, we'd all love you to come". So I told myself, "Oh sod it, I'll go". I was thinking, "I'm in pain most of the time anyway so why not do something to earn it!" So I did go, and to be honest it was pretty uncomfortable because the chairs were a bad style for me, but I did enjoy talking to people outside of work. And even just getting dressed up somehow made me feel a bit more like the old me. I did pay for it the next couple of days, I knew I would. But Dave was really helpful and told me it was worth it to see me having enjoyed myself. Made me feel even closer to Dave that did.

Questions to explore what may be absent but implicit

Can you tell me more about this feeling of (anger, upset, despair, worry, failure)?

When is it around? How often? And how long for?

What do you think this feeling relates to? For example, is (this feeling) telling you that something is not fair? That something has been violated? Crushed? Pushed around? Lost? Or that you are missing something?

What does the presence of this feeling, and experiencing it so strongly, tell you about what you value? Consider important? What you might be standing up for? Not going along with? Or hoping to reconnect with?

Might this feeling be considered a response to injustice/a violation/a sense of missing? Or how have you responded to this, what action have you taken, even if this is just quietly questioning this in your head?

What feels important for you in your management of this illness? Your relationship to it? Or how you would prefer your treatment/medical care to be organised?

Step three: making the (seemingly) small significant

Returning to all the material that has now been pulled together with a person, a therapist will likely have various events or descriptions possibly indicative of a unique outcome. The focus of this step is to work out which, if any, are important. However, if asked straight away, when an event still seems small and inconsequential, a person can often respond with a "no, it is not". Thus, it is important to engage in a practice known as "thickening" and to further explore the meaning of each event. This enables a person to have more information to draw on before they reach their conclusion (White, 1995). We would now like to introduce you to two "landscapes" that can be helpful in this process.

The "landscape of action" and "landscape of identity" (White, 2007)

The "landscape of action" orientates therapists to what is actually known about a person's situation, for example, what are they doing, have done, or would like to do. It refers to concrete actions such as: Jennifer gave her brother a hug, Susan did not take her medication, or Tom disclosed thinking about his wife in hospital. The "landscape of identity", by contrast, considers the meaning of any such initiative, in terms of what it may speak of about a person's hopes and values. Thus, what initially may seem like just a hug could also indicate that Jennifer values being there for those important to her. Hence her embracing other people is an expression of caring and support. It might also lead to discussion about the importance, for Jennifer, of "having someone in her corner" and her ability to offer that to others. For Susan, the decision not to take her medication and try alternative therapies may have followed a period of extensive reading and research. It is an action potentially indicative of the importance of choice for Susan, and to be in control of decisions made about her life and health. Tom's action, by comparison, highlights his capacity to distract himself and hold on to such images, despite experiencing a lot of pain. There are skills in his ability to do this, but the choosing to think about his wife might reflect the importance to him of being her husband.

Conversations guided by these two landscapes can support a therapist with the task of building meaning. Yet facilitating the movement

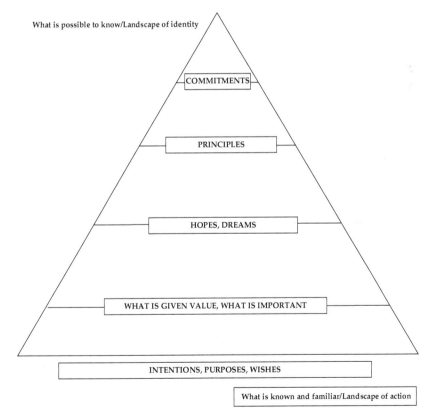

Figure 2.1. Fox's slope or ladder of intentional state identity categories (Fox, 2008).

from what a concrete action says about a person and their hopes in life is often quite a leap for the therapist to assist a person in making. There are, however, ways to scaffold such a conversation and for the conversation to travel in both directions. Fox's ladder (2008) is a tool that specifically addresses this question. It does this by first focusing a therapist on the intention behind a deed, and then with each rung, questions incrementally increase in distance to allow more abstract ideas and concepts to be discussed.

The latter categories of the ladder (if a therapist travels in the direction of action to identity) considers what a person's conduct might mean in terms of what they would like to stand for as a person, how they would like to be seen, or what knowledge they already possess to tackle the predicament at hand. Travelling in the other direction, from identity to action, a person is encouraged to think about how these realisations translate into what can actually be done, steps they would like to take, or ideas they wish to hold on to. There is no expectation to follow the rungs in a linear fashion. Indeed, therapists should listen out for "I don't know" answers as these can often signal when they might need to take a step down, reframe the question, or spend more time exploring.

Some ideas for questions to explore Fox's slope:

Intentions/purposes/wishes: What were you thinking about when you made the choice to do this? What made you take this action and not another? What helped you do this? What knowledge and/or skills did you draw on? And where did you learn these from?

Values/what's important: What do you think taking this action, and for this reason, says about what you consider important or what matters to you? Why did it feel important to do this and in this way?

Hopes/dreams: What do these actions/values say about your hopes for your life? What do these values say about your dreams for your life, for others, the world?

Principles: In what ways do these hopes extend to broader hopes about how things could be? What feels important for you about the way in which we all live our lives, are there certain principles or ethics that you would like to remember? What do these principles say about what you are trying to stand up for?

Commitments: What values /ways of living would you like to stay connected to/keep hold of? What difference would keeping these ideas close to you make? (e.g., in your life, work, relationships)

Suzanne—some examples of beginning to build meaning

Together, we explored seemingly small acts that appeared inconsistent with Suzanne's dominant problem story, seeking in each case to encourage her to recognise the intention(s) and broader meaning behind each. For example:

- Suzanne would sometimes close her bedroom door and put her face in a pillow when crying "so the kids don't hear me". Her intentions in this action being to protect the children from worry and stress, and to enable them to see their mother as able to cope.
- Suzanne would always make her partner a cup of tea when he came home, despite the pain she was in. Her intentions were to show him that she valued him, in a way that she was able to, to create a space for them to talk, and as a physical act of caring.
- Suzanne would switch her phone to a different mode so that it didn't send an acknowledgement to the sender after reading a text. Her intentions were to give herself "breathing space" by putting off the need to respond to her sister's unpleasant messages, to reclaim some control for herself, and not let her sister dictate and intrude, and to avoid "giving in".

Evaluating significance

It is at this point, following the expansion of meaning, that the significance of each event can be explored. Yet doing so requires a therapist to remain mindful of his or her own ideas and values in order to ensure that it is the person's experience, knowledge, skills that are privileged and not those of the therapist.

> It can be tempting, as a therapist, to fill this gap with my own knowledge and there are a million small ways to do this, mostly ways which subtly or not so subtly try to align other people's lives and understandings with my own. These ways can include giving advice or support a particular perspective. Or they may involve giving implicit advice—advice disguised as questions, wonderings or tasks.

(Hayward, 2006, p. 1)

Within medical settings, it can be surprisingly easy to steer a person towards better conforming to norms expected of them by their team. Thus the therapist needs to also remain vigilant that conversations do not simply replicate or reproduce dominant cultural stories. Conversations that approach the issue of significance carefully, however, will often yield several unique outcomes that a person is interested in exploring further.

Some ideas for questions to explore possible significance:

Is this something that you have thought about?
Are you surprised to hear that you took this action for these reasons?
Who would have appreciated you taking this action? Who wouldn't be surprised?
Were you aware that you did this?
What do you think about this?
Is this something that you would like to think more about?

Step four: linking and connecting further

Having lain for weeks, or sometimes years, unnoticed in the shadow of the problem story, unique outcomes tend to be quite fragile. The focus of the previous step has been to increase their visibility by building meaning and evaluating their significance. Yet for unique outcomes to become stronger still, they need to be connected to an even greater degree. Narrative theory depicts stories as events linked over time, and according to a particular plot or theme. As previously stated, careful listening and noting any (potentially) linked unique outcomes is a recommended starting point to re-authoring.

Mark Hayward's scaffolding distance map (2006) is a framework that, together with the practice of editorialising (White, 2007), can be helpful at this point. Similar to Fox's ladder, it considers ways in which a person may move from problem stories to preferred accounts. Yet it differs in that the focus is more on connecting and exploring multiple unique outcomes rather than just one. The map has eight categories. The first relates to describing the "problem experience" which has been covered in Chapter One, while the second talks about the identification of "exceptional experience" which has also been thought about. Thus the stages to consider next are outlined in the table below.

Stage	Description	Example and possible questions
Misnaming and naming	• The practice of naming supports exploration and clarification of the problem story: it also forms part of externalisation. • Misnaming can be useful as it is usually easier to first decide what something is not. • As with problem accounts, naming will tend to change with time. It important to continue checking that the name still fits. • Editorialising is the process by which a therapist summarises all of the initiatives that have been noticed. Presenting information in this way can help facilitate evaluation and meaning-making.	• You have talked about HIV feeling like an "assault" on your sense of self as a person, and that in response you have taken steps to try to make HIV a very small part of your life. • You have talked about your developing interest in gardening and spending time on the allotment. • You also note that you do not make specific attempts to seek out other people who are positive, not that you actively avoid people who are, but that you find yourself simply trying to continue with life without defining yourself in a particular way. • What would you call these steps that you have taken? (i.e., after thinking about this, Joseph began to refer to these steps as "The Plan"). • Does this sound like a name that fits for you? If yes, why do you think so? If no, what is it that does not sound right?
Bringing things into relationship	• Here, the focus is on the explicit linking between one outcome and other events that speak of something similar.	• Can you tell me about other times in your life when you have done this or something similar? (i.e., Joseph identified not going to groups at a local charity and not ascribing to the view that you have to be "positive about being [HIV] positive")

Figure2.2. Continued

	• The therapist encourages a person to think about ways in which these events may be linked or different, as well as their social and relational history. • As part of this process, a therapist may find themselves travelling forwards as well as backwards in time. Gathering moments that have occurred as far back as a person's childhood, or going forward by anticipating actions that may occur in future.	• In what way do you think these actions are linked? (i.e., Joseph felt they too came under the broader response, referred to as "The Plan") • Who knew this about you? Or would be least surprised to know this? Who has contributed to you being able to do this? • What skills are involved in the Plan, what do you draw on that helps you with this? Where did you learn these from, when did you first find yourself being able to do this?
Reflections on life and identity	• Connections are explored further by encouraging a person to think about what these relationships might mean for them. • So what certain initiatives might say about what a person values or considers precious, their hopes for how they would like to live their life or be seen by others.	• What does this skill, hope, belief, initiative say about what matters to you as a person? (i.e., it was identified that "The Plan" was Joseph's attempt to reconnect himself with those things that he valued and that sustained him. He reflected that he valued having a rich and diverse life, being surrounded by interesting people and involved in activities that interested him. He also noted that he wanted a career that he found rewarding, to have a husband, as well as take pleasure from the simple things in life)

Figure2.2. Continued

		• What does this say about how you would like to be seen? (i.e., he identified that he was actively resisting being seen in a particular way just because he was diagnosed as living with HIV) • How long have these values been important to you? (i.e., Joseph identified that these things had been important from his teenage years) Where did you first learn about them, and who would be supportive of them?
Founda-tions for action	• At this point, a person is supported to reflect on how they wish to go on in life and con-template—do I wish to go on in this way or another? • As a person becomes clearer about their pre-ferred hopes, ideas for what they can actually do often become easier to think about.	• Thinking about what you have reflected on as impor-tant, what has it left you thinking in terms of how you wish to go forward in life? • Is there anything that you would like to stay the same, keep hold of, or be different? If the latter, what would you like to do more of or less of? (i.e., Joseph identified that he wanted to continue to hold on to this sense of himself) • Do you have any ideas about how you may be able to do this? (i.e., remembering this conversation and continuing to pursue diverse activities, taking up opportunities that interest him as and when they came along)

Figure 2.2. Continued

| Problem-solving | • The person is encouraged to reflect on what concrete actions can be taken to make these realisations and ideas possible.
• This might include trouble-shooting what could get in the way of or cause a problem, how they might be able to side-step current concerns, alongside what or whom might be able to support them to do this. | • How do these knowledges, skills, realisations support you when you think about the problem at hand? (i.e., Joseph reflected that, although HIV had seemed an assault on his personhood, he had actually found ways to resist this and reduce its effects)
• What do you know that you can draw on or that might support you to have a slightly different relationship to the problem? Or does the concern still feel a problem for you?
• What do you know that might help you cope with it? (i.e., again Joseph reflected that he had already taken a number of steps to support a different view of himself, a view he preferred, and was continuing to do so, for example, he was planning to get further involved in gardening, another diverse interest)
• Who could you recruit to help you hold on to this position? How might they be able to help? How can you let them know this? (i.e., Joseph reflected that, for him, seeking support from his existing social network was important, many of whom were friends who were not HIV positive, and for them to remain unaware of his status) |

Figure 2.2. Stage 3–7 based on Mark Hayward's scaffolding distance map.

Step five: thickening preferred stories

This intentional process of connecting unique outcomes will likely have resulted in at least one, but hopefully multiple, alternative stories at a therapist's disposal. Stories are "stronger" than unique outcomes, yet "freshly developing stories [are still] vulnerable" (Cooper, 2014, p. 24), for without a context that supports their re-telling and circulation, they can be easily cast aside. Narrative theory argues that it is predominately through others hearing, acknowledging, and sharing alternative stories that their resilience and capacity for influence can increase. This practice is referred to as "re-telling" (White, 2007) or "witnessing" (Fredman, 2014; Freedman, 2014), and there are many ways in which this can be done.

One example is to use documents to capture particular conversations: Chapter Seven thinks about this further. Another relates to the actual getting together of people to listen to a person's story. This is known as "outsider witnessing" (White, 2007) and involves recruiting a selected audience to hear, and ideally thicken, a preferred account of life and identity. In addition to developing an even richer description, simply having others bear witness can support relationships more sustaining of it. When a therapist works within a health setting, an outsider-witnessing group has the potential to be made up of a person's medical team (if appropriate). Yet it is not always easy or practical to formally bring people together; instead, questions can be asked to capture witnesses and resonances from team members as and when they are able to offer them.

Some ideas for questions to support appreciative witnessing by members of the team:

What do they/have they appreciated about a person?

What have they noticed or observed? (i.e., for example, in their management of their condition, their interests, their relationships with the team/their family)?

What has surprised them most in their interactions with them?

In what way have their interactions potentially influenced their work or views?

Cooper (2014, p. 24) also makes reference to enquiring before meeting, "What might I come to know and appreciate about the person if I had time to get to know about them?".

Step six: developing contexts that sustain preferred stories

Thus far, this chapter has focused on a person's preferred story, but it is important to remember that each person will be situated within a broader context still.

Becoming aware of this is essential, in that surrounding systems have the potential to squeeze or expand space available for preferred stories to be heard. Even the decision to refer will have tapped into stories a team may have, for example, about what a "good" chronic pain patient does, how the service should operate, and what health workers feel is expected of them. Consequently, whenever we try to bring preferred accounts to the fore, there is always the potential that they may conflict with existing stories held by the service. Yet unlike other settings, therapists working within health services are often based within the same department. This physical positioning offers the opportunity to do something more, as the therapist has direct access to the team!

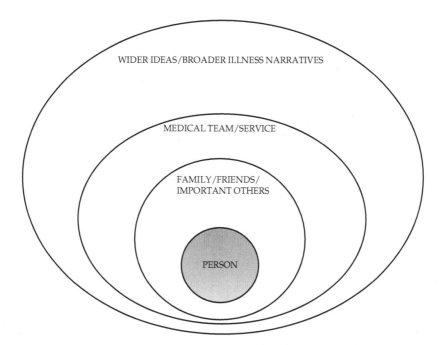

Figure 2.3. Diagram to highlight the multiple systems in which a person is based.

And with this, the potential to jointly consider and renegotiate ways of working that are supportive of people's preferred stories and, ideally, the teams also.

Sustaining preferred identity

Suzanne came to see that an alternative view of her life was possible; in fact, that many alternative views of her life were possible: Suzanne as a skilled organiser, planner, and prioritiser: Suzanne as a committed Mum: Suzanne as compassionate and thoughtful: Suzanne as fun-loving and funny.

With permission, I shared these alternative stories of Suzanne and the strategies she had developed to help her cope with the pain. For example, managing her energy resources to ensure that she could prioritise what she would really like to do (a pain team suggested technique)—DNA-ing appointments was, therefore, one way of preserving energy to accomplish far more important things to her, like making a World Book Day costume for her daughter.

At times when she had sought higher levels of medication, it had been when she had been refusing to allow The Boss to stop her from doing something that was important to her. While she reported now finding ways of doing this that didn't involve increasing her medication, which on the whole she preferred as it reduced the side effects she could experience, the intention in requesting more medication was in itself an attempt by Suzanne to wrest back some degree of control from her pain condition (another pain team suggested approach).

Through sharing some of Suzanne's initiatives alongside alternative stories of her as a person and what mattered to her in life, her relationship with the pain team began to change. There was a developing mutual openness to considering each other's intentions and hopes behind their actions, which had not previously existed. As a result, Suzanne attended (and subsequently reported having enjoyed and got lots from) the pain team group programme for learning approaches to living well with chronic pain. As part of the group, Suzanne developed a flare-up plan (an advanced statement for how to deal with episodes when the pain gets worse). Suzanne felt confident to pro-actively take this to her GP (with whom she had previously had a difficult relationship) and to tell him that this is how she would like to proceed at such times. She was able to successfully negotiate his agreement to adhere to the plan at such times.

Suzanne told me that the change in her relationships with the pain team and with her GP had helped solidify her view of herself as someone who could be competent, organised, skilled at prioritising and negotiating, and someone who was "equal to dealing with medical people" where previously she had felt intimidated and offended.

My own experience of the changes in the view of Suzanne from "the system" was encouraging too. I saw and heard both the team and her GP change the language used to talk about Suzanne and bring a new level of willingness to be open to her preferences for care, where previously this had been limited. Whenever I had the opportunity (in team meetings, letters, and office discussions), I would attempt to thicken these new ideas of Suzanne and challenge any slipping back to the earlier, less helpful views.

Over time and the many people I have worked with, these approaches began to take root in the system (a little) and, to my infinite pleasure, I found my own slip-ups into less helpful ways of thinking about clients (we all have those moments, I flatter myself) being challenged by the team, who had learned to appreciate a more open approach to understanding the people with whom we work. I strongly believe that this gentle spreading of ideas, use of language and approaches can have a big impact, and help sustain narrative approaches within these environments.

One final point: "consulting your consultants" (Epston & White, 1990)

This practice "serves to shift the status of a person from client to consultant" (Madigan, p. 7). It acknowledges that each and every person that a therapist meets will have unique knowledge and skills about how to deal with a particular concern(s). This "insider knowledge can be documented and made available to others struggling with similar issues" (Madigan, p. 7; Madigan & Epston, 1995).

Some examples of questions to encourage reflection:

Given your expertise in managing the effects of living with multiple sclerosis, what have you learned that might be useful for others to be aware of?

As an old hand at living with uncertainty, what tips or suggestions can you offer to those beginning their journey with this feeling?

As someone living with hepatitis C, and with your knowledge of the tactics "Shame" and "Stigma" can try to use to affect how you see/feel about yourself, what might you want others to know or think about when facing similar problems?

Once gathered, and with permission, there are many creative ways in which this information can be passed on. For example, it can be made into a collective document or leaflet that others attending the service could access. Notes or messages could be pinned to a board in the waiting room. Markey (2015), in her work with young people, described the novel idea of a "graffitied tree" which enabled a "collection of words attached to foliage" and "at the end of each branch dangles skills and instructions, phrases and poems from other students who are keen to pass on their knowledge" (Markey, 2015, p. 4). For example, it included ideas about "how to talk about death", "how to say sorry", and "what to do when you're new at school" (Markey, 2015, p. 4).

Another lovely example comes from Gerlitz (2015), who anonymously joined two people with whom she was working through letter writing, both of which had experience and knowledge of living with chronic pain. In addition to creating space where knowledge about what helped them cope could be passed on, this practice facilitated the linking of lives and for each to possibly feel less isolated in their experience. Gerlitz supported their letter writing by asking specific questions, as well as using the correspondence from the other as a means of further reflection within sessions.

In conclusion

The aim of this chapter has been to encourage you (as the therapist) to have a go at re-authoring! The steps described may have been numbered for convenience, but there is no expectation for them to be followed in the order outlined. You might find, for example, that information gathered at step four (linking and connecting) helps you identify further unique outcomes (step two) or to find out more about a person still (step one). Moreover, while the conclusions reached within the example appear to have been reached within a relatively short time period, we would like to reassure you that this was not the case. This is not to say that narrative ideas cannot be used when time is limited, but it is our experience that often considerable time is spent building back up to points previously reached. This might be because something has happened in between meetings that appears to have undermined a person's connection to the new (or even old) ideas that they were coming to, or that the problem story had been doing its job well and a person has forgotten.

We consider the primary role of a therapist, therefore, to be the one who keeps hold of all the various conversational strands, returning to them at points to build meaning and enquire as to their significance. Expect to lose your way and, rather than allowing hopelessness to capture you, instead hold on to the idea that getting lost can be fun and may lead you to some unexpected places. Moreover, if you always endeavour to stay with the person and centre their knowledge, you can never truly get lost.

Acknowledgements

Rachel would like to thank: those who have consulted with her, and offered to share their own stories to support others; Hugh Fox and Sarah Walther, who introduced her to narrative approaches; other members and attendees at courses and summer schools of the UK Institute of Narrative Therapy; the members of Hugh Fox's Manchester Narrative Supervision group; Louise Mozo-Dutton for believing in her and inviting her to contribute to this book, especially her patient editorial support; and lastly, she would like to thank her insightful and wonderful husband Stephen for his unwavering support, encouragement, and intelligent advice. Everyone in this list has supported Rachel in her journey into using narrative therapy and contributed to her learning and development in this area.

Louise would like to thank the people who have been kind enough to allow their story to be shared. Many thanks also to Rachel, for all of our conversations and especially her ability to keep this chapter (and me) on track.

References

Cooper, S. (2014). Brief narrative practice at the walk-in clinic: the rise of the counter story. *The International Journal of Narrative Therapy and Community Work, 2*: 23–30.

Derrida, J. (1978). *Writing and Difference.* London: Routledge.

Epston, D., & White, M. (1990). Consulting your consultants: the documentation of alternative knowledges. *Dulwich Centre Newsletter, 4*: 25–35.

Fox, H. (2008). *Level 1 Narrative Training: A Four Day Course (Notes).* Manchester: Centre for Narrative Practice.

Fredman, G. (2014). Weaving networks of hope with families, practitioners and communities: inspirations from systemic and narrative approaches. *The International Journal of Narrative Therapy and Community Work, 1*: 34–44.

Freedman, J. (2014). Witnessing and positioning: structuring narrative therapy with families and couples. *The International Journal of Narrative Therapy and Community Work, 1*: 11–17.

Gerlitz, J. (2015). Linking lives: invitations to clients to write letters to clients. *The International Journal of Narrative Therapy and Community Work, 3*: 44–54.

Hayward, M. (2006). Using a scaffolding distance map with a young man and his family. http://www.theinstituteofnarrativetherapy.com/Using%20Michael%20Whites%20Scaffoldin g%20Distance%20Map.pdf (accessed 13 February).

Madigan, S. (no date given). Madigan Handouts TC9: Vancouver Narrative Therapy Training. http://therapeuticconversations.com/wp-content/uploads/2010/01/Handout_Madigan_Reauthoring_TC9-.pdf (accessed 20 February).

Madigan, S., & Epston, D. (1995). From "spy-chiatric gaze" to communities of concern: from professional monologue to dialogue. In: S. Friedman (Ed.), *The Reflecting Team in Action: Collaborative Practice in Family Therapy* (pp. 257–276). New York: Guilford.

Markey, C. (2015). Exploring feminist narrative practice and ethics in a school setting. *The International Journal of Narrative Therapy and Community Work, 4*: 1–10.

McGoldrick, M., Gerson, R., & Shellenberger, S. (1999). *Genograms: Assessment and Intervention.* New York: W. W. Norton.

Russell, S., & Carey, M. (2002). Re-membering: commonly asked questions. http://narrativepractices.com.au/attach/pdf/Remembering_Common_Questions.pdf (accessed 17 January).

Simchon, M. (2013). Words from the brink of the chasm. *The International Journal of Narrative Therapy and Community Work, 1:* 1–7.

White, M. (1995). *Re-Authoring Lives: Interviews and Essays.* Adelaide: Dulwich Centre.

White, M. (2000). Re-engaging with history: the absent but implicit. In: M. White (Ed.), *Reflections on Narrative Practice* (pp. 35–57). Adelaide: Dulwich Centre.

White, M. (2005). Children, trauma and subordinate storyline development. *The International Journal of Narrative Therapy and Community* Work, *3 & 4:* 10–21.

White, M. (2007). *Maps of Narrative Practice.* New York: W. W. Norton.

White, M., & Epston, D. (1990). Story, knowledge and power. In: M. White & D. Epston (Eds.), *Narrative Means to Therapeutic Ends* (pp. 1–37). Adelaide: Dulwich Centre.

Winslade, J., & Hedkte, L. (2008). Michael White: fragments of an event. *The International Journal of Narrative Therapy and Community Work, 2:* 5–11.

CHAPTER THREE

Discourse and narratives of illness

Jennifer Pomfret and Lincoln Simmonds

This chapter is organised into two parts. Part one examines the philosophical and theoretical underpinnings to the use of discourse within narrative therapy. Part two highlights the application of narrative therapy in relation to discourse, and this section is peppered with examples of using these practices with people.

Part one: the philosophical and theoretical background to working with discourse

Narrative therapy works with the stories of people's lives, and the meanings that people assign to these discourses. There are many definitions of this concept of discourse. One possibility offered by Vivien Burr (1995) that particularly fits with the narrative therapy approach states that, "Discourse refers to a set of meanings, metaphors, representations, images, stories, statements and so on that in some way together produce a particular version of events" (Vivien Burr, 1995, p. 11).

As previous chapters have explored, some discourses or stories are more privileged within society. Discourses that are more broadly preferred or widely circulated are thus more dominant, whereas other stories and discourses can lie untold or unsupported. This can cause difficulties where there is an apparent disconnect or conflict between the dominant discourse of an illness and a person's own perceived experience of it. It may be the case that the person is not yet fully aware of how they wish to story their lives. They have a sense nonetheless that the prevailing ideas about how to experience, manage, or cope with their illness do not work well for them.

Narrative therapy is a form of noticing and acknowledging when discourse may have become problematic. Narrative therapy uses maps and categories of questions that actively support the deconstruction of such ideas—including how they may have reached their current level of dominance. From this position, a person can be supported to consider in which ways these ideas are useful to them, or how the ideas might have got in the way of what they want for their life. This process often leads to the identification and thickening of lesser-told stories which fit better with the person's hopes and values. The process also involves the development of rich accounts of how an individual has been able to live their life in preferred ways, despite the problematic accounts.

> As a therapist working in physical health with a long-term physical health condition (one of the authors in this chapter), I have witnessed from both a personal and professional perspective how useful it can be to use ideas from narrative therapy to story my own personal experience. I was diagnosed with rheumatoid arthritis at the age of eighteen months and grew up often needing to use a wheelchair. I found talking about my health condition as a child an incredibly difficult conversation to have with people. I frequently experienced flare-ups of my condition, and often had to adjust plans as a result of this. I developed a name for speaking about the effects of arthritis, and named it Arthur. I found that cancelling or adjusting plans because Arthur was "playing up" was a lot easier for me to admit to and speak about, than saying I could not do something because I was in pain or could not physically manage. Without knowing it, I had begun to experiment with some basic narrative ideas by naming the effects of the problem and using the technique of externalisation.

Dominant psychotherapeutic ideas of how to work with people with physical health concerns can come from the perspective of emphasising the need to "challenge" the problem. At times, workers can receive referrals relating to individuals being fearful of a recurrence of their illness. It might be the case that people are checking their bodies on a regular basis for growths or tumours. Challenging these thoughts or beliefs by encouraging a person to evaluate the "reality" of them, "change" or "restructure" them, or perhaps refrain from these checking behaviours can seem inadequate and perhaps inappropriate. This fear, for example, might be referred to as "irrational" and a person thought to be "catastrophising" their current circumstances. They may be viewed as placing too much emphasis on their past experiences or viewing their situation too simplistically. However, for the person, a fear of the illness returning or their condition worsening following a life-threatening diagnosis cannot really be called irrational. Yet such practices can, at times, fit with dominant discourses of how people with a physical health problem "should be", or perhaps how we "should work" with people in therapy. Narrative therapy offers a different approach, one in which a person is supported to see alternative or even multiple stories specific to themselves, any one of which may feel more useful and helpful to their lived experience. So, for example, the person may develop a story about the checking behaviours being a way of looking after themselves. They may then be interested in looking at other ways of looking after themselves, which might develop more space for other important areas of their life outside of the checking behaviours.

In order to understand this further, it is important to acknowledge where narrative therapy has come from. The next section of this chapter provides an overview as to the philosophical underpinnings of the model.

Modernism, structuralism, and the concept of self

Modernism generally describes a period towards the end of the eighteenth century when an ideological shift occurred. It is argued to have begun in the West, and is often referred to as the Age of Enlightenment (Fox, 1993). A new way of viewing the world developed, and the study of human sciences commenced. A modernist view of people and their behaviour is that it can be measured, grouped, and labelled in order to better understand the human experience. It is from this discourse that the notion of "self" developed, and in particular the idea that each person is in possession of a "true self". This concept puts forward a view that, through investigation, the parts believed to make up our true self can be identified; and that these parts are predictable in that they are considered relatively stable and unchanging over time. This concept has been readily integrated within our culture, and, for many, the idea of a "true or core self" can feel comforting. It offers a framework by which we can make sense of our varied experiences in life. It also encourages a sense of "knowing ourselves and knowing the selves of others" in that we have an idea about how we, or someone else, may react in a particular situation or set of circumstances. This concept can therefore offer a sense of personal continuity.

Yet beliefs that a person possesses a true self can also place limits on whom we might envisage ourselves to be at any one time or in any situation. It can also limit how much a person is thought to be able to change across context and time. These beliefs can affect how people might come to describe problems, the language they and others use, and the beliefs that surround how such a problem may have come into existence. Hence a person can hold the view that a problem is a reflection of failing to their true self. They may thus view the problem as being within them and reflective of a "disorder", "deficit", or particular form of "damage" (Carey & Russell, 2004). Yet how can workers then reconcile their knowledge and experience of people changing, if this view were to be wholly accepted? How does a "true self" change; and especially if a true self is believed to contain some form of inherent damage within it?

The philosophy of structuralism is intimately connected to the modernist era. This was developed in the early nineteenth century and refers to a belief that, under the surface of everything, there is a structure that can be studied and understood. Practitioners influenced by these ideas aimed to study and analyse each and every component in order to discover how components are linked, and what each part does. In many respects, this has proven a useful concept; for example, science has developed theories about structures, atoms, and genetics that have helped develop new technologies and treatments. Structuralist theories were also used to develop the disciplines of psychology and psychiatry. Theories argued that people could be studied and understood in terms of structures, and perceived "truths" often referred to as "facts". Thus, if an individual was struggling to cope, or was behaving in ways that differed to what was considered appropriate or normal, then it was believed there was something wrong with the individual's underlying structures.

Traditional psychoanalysis, which has been developed and adapted over time, was based on this premise and utilised techniques that sought to bring the problem, often thought located deep within the self, to the surface. Freud referred to this process as bringing the problem into an individual's consciousness rather than allowing it to remain repressed or hidden (Freud, 1896). Terminology used within such structuralist approaches has included drives, traits, needs, disorders, and rigid or internalised thinking. This language and way of speaking about difficulties implies that these problems are within an individual, with less emphasis placed upon external factors or contributing environmental explanations, other than the idea that inherent difficulties are thought to have developed in conjunction with early childhood experiences, or a single event or aspect of a person's life (e.g., a trauma or a relationship with a significant person). The structuralist approach also implicitly states that in order to address a problem, we need the help of "experts". These experts are viewed as having specialist knowledge about problems and what they believe to help, which can be privileged over what a person knows.

Structuralist viewpoints certainly have their place in the world. This perspective has helped to improve and advance what we know of as science and therapy. Many therapists use these ideas to highlight as well as work with distress, with great success. There are many structuralist-based therapies that the National Institute for Health and Care Excellence (NICE) guidelines would recommend for many difficulties or diagnoses, and thus the use of structuralist techniques has supported many people to move forward with their lives. The question remains, though: What if working with someone from a structuralist approach is not a good fit for a person's problems and their lived experience?

Power

Structuralist explanations of problems are helpful when they are consistent with what the person finds useful to them. This is often determined less by the structuralist account uncovering some absolute "truth" about the person; rather, the therapist is interested in how the person "views" the structuralist account as being able to help them move towards their own preferred direction of change. For those for whom this is not the case (and they have no other alternative explanations available to them), these ideas may lead a person to overly attribute difficulties to something lacking within themselves. Hence, they may consider themselves damaged, or to be failures in living life "correctly". These ideas link heavily with a discourse of individualism, which promotes the view that both perceived "success" as well as "failure" are the sole responsibilities of the individual. Thus, where a person fails to meet what is expected of them, other factors, such as poverty or reduced opportunities potentially linked to systemic inequality, may be glossed over or not even considered.

This point leads us on to the thorny issue of power, and the intimate relationship it is believed to have with discourse and ideas privileged. This relationship is one that embodied a life's work for the French philosopher Michel Foucault. White and Epston in their development of narrative therapy drew greatly from Foucault, and in particular his ideas on modern power (Foucault, 1980; White & Epston, 1989). Foucault conceptualised two forms of power that he considered in operation within society today. The first, traditional power, describes power held by particular individuals or groups that is used to serve the interests of the system at the subjugation of all others. Examples of this can be seen in countries where there is a dictatorship in place. This form of power is often visible to those enveloped by it, as well as by those that stand outside of it. Yet despite visibility, the strong threat of reprisal tends to mean that most will feel fearful of resisting the ways of living prescribed by the system.

Yet the world has witnessed a shift from societies governed by traditional models of power to democracy, where citizens are described as equal and encouraged to play a part in how their country is run. Within democratic states, the role of punishment to enforce social control has lessened but in its place norms have arisen. This form of power, modern power, is one that "recruits people into the active participation of fashioning their own lives, their relationships and their identities, according to the constructed norms of culture" (White, 2002, p. 36). Structuralist and modernist theories of self have, therefore, been especially instrumental in supporting the development of a "set of normalising truths which have the power to shape our lives and relationships" (Walther & Carey, 2009, p. 3). Thus what "we" (the people) consider normal is now the principal means by which society is organised and our own behaviour regulated, as well as the behaviour of others. Modern power is subtle and less easily observed than traditional power and, thus, has been described as "insidious" and "pervasive" in its operations (White, 2002, p. 36). Foucault was intent on exposing "the extent to which we had become unwitting instruments" in the reproduction and maintenance of particular ways of living. He believed that becoming more aware of how modern power operates is the first step to beginning to undermine the process itself (White, 2002, p. 36).

In 2002, White reflected on how awareness of the workings of modern power could have the effect of separating people from feelings of hopefulness; yet he drew attention to the idea that "systems of power are very rarely, if ever total, in their effects" as well as entirely "dependent upon people's active participation" with them (White, 2002, p. 36). Thus, he argued that there would always be opportunities for a person, group, or community to engage in acts of resistance. Further narrative conversations are one means by which even small acts "might be rendered more visible, richly known [and] acknowledged" (White, 2002, p. 36), and in doing so, space can be opened for a different conversation (less restricted by modern power) to be had.

Social constructionism, non-structuralism, and the concept of identity

Narrative therapy might, therefore, be considered a therapy that has developed in response to modernist and structuralist ways of viewing the world. It is often seen as a counter perspective referred to as post-structuralism. Post-structuralist philosophers believe that meaning is iterative and subjective, and therefore dependent upon societal, cultural, and historical factors. Post-structuralism is a philosophy closely connected with the concept of social constructionism. This is a term first introduced by Berger and Luckmann (1966) when they published *The Social Construction of Reality*, and used the term to refer to a trend or phenomenon that is formed or created as a result of social processes; thus predominately through language.

Thinking about these ideas in relation to personhood and the experience of distress, the emphasis more clearly shifts to "meaning made" as opposed to what "we are believed to be". These philosophies actively resist the idea that we can arrive at a particular truth about the world or indeed ourselves. Instead, this position views facts as information agreed as true by several people or groups, and often those who occupy powerful or privileged positions. They re-focus our attention on how we construct meaning, and how we develop linguistic frameworks to support us in this process. Frameworks, it could be argued, that are entirely dependent on language, and forever being negotiated and renegotiated "between people". Moreover, such constructions are not believed to be passive, but rather as White and Foucault's reflections on norms highlight, formative in their effects also.

We do not wish to suggest that one philosophy is right while another is wrong, but we have found perspectives developed from non-structuralist and social constructionist ideas to be particularly freeing within the therapeutic context. Rather than viewing problems as inter-nal, thinking of them as constructed allows a person to reconstruct or change how much emphasis they wish to place on these ideas. Rather than a true self, non-structuralist accounts place greater emphasis on intentions, values, hopes, wishes, commitments, and principles. They refer to this sense of ourselves as "identity": a concept that can incorpo-rate a sense of stability if a person so wishes, but also allows for change in that we are no longer "bound to who we feel we are" but rather the question shifts towards "whom do we wish to become?" (Walther & Carey, 2009, p. 4); "Different possibilities for identity [can therefore be] opened up by revising our relationships with problems, discourses and people" (Redstone, Fox, Gorney, & Ord, 2012, p. 2). Thus, while still remaining mindful of wider restraints and factors at play, people are considered active agents with the capacity to make changes within their own lives.

Narrative therapy therefore assumes that meaning is developed and perpetuated in the telling and re-telling of our stories (Bruner, 1990). Narratives are said to be embodied by both "perspective" and "content" (Gee, 1991). Perspective refers to a set of events an individ-ual has experienced, while content refers to the meaning developed around those events; or as White & Epston (1990) note, narratives comprise events linked over time and according to a particular plot or theme. Personal narratives are powerful in that they are considered the principal means by which people interpret, understand, speak of, and relive key moments within their lives and the lives of others (Squire, 2005). Narrative therapy aims to support individuals to make sense of their experiences in ways that feel helpful for them (Langellier, 2001). White (2007) also documents the benefit of storytelling but in a "deliberate" and "particular" way. Thus, a therapist can explore a problem in relation to a person's life story and contextualise it by con-sidering its varying influence across time, events, relationships, and situations. This process opens up space for re-authoring conversations, whereby people are then encouraged to re-describe their experience to strengthen particular and preferred accounts of identity and living. This is in contrast to people feeling tied to accounts that may have been defined for them by others.

A brief summary

So how do these ideas apply to working with people with physical health problems? Ideas from modernism and structuralism underpin many of the discourses about how to live life well with a physical health problem. The dominance of these discourses is maintained through the wide circulation of particular stories, written explanations, or communications regularly had within health settings. Engaging in discussions with a person or medical team that simply reproduce ideas about how to live with a physical health concern may be unhelpful, as it may serve only to reinforce a sense of what is the norm in these situations (Kierans & Maynooth, 2001). Narrative therapy, by contrast, offers opportunities to construct a *self-authored* and *experience-near* story or discourse about a person's particular lived experience; stories that are hoped to fit better with a person's specific context, history, and relationships, rather than generalised stories of how people should apparently cope or manage.

Discourse relating to illness

Weingarten (2001, p. 1), in her personal reflections, made reference to her commitment to "bring into awareness narratives of illness, disability, medical disorders, chronic conditions, genetic disorders, disease, dying and death". This statement highlights the sheer number of ideas about bodies and, more specifically, unreliable bodies that are readily available within our culture. In relation to problems that affect bodies, the discourse of capitalism might be considered particularly influential in recent years. This discourse leans heavily on other related concepts such as individualism and self already discussed. Such ideas accord status and allow for the differentiation between positions deemed worthy and of value, and those less so. In order to live within these ideas, a person is usually in need of a reliable body, and one that enables them to perform to the best of their abilities and at all times (Weingarten, 2001).

In addition to more general ideas relating to illness, wellness, success, and personal worth, people's personal stories of illness usually link with wider ideas held within our culture about the condition in question (Conrad & Barker, 2010). Thus, each illness will come with different social constructs, culture, and meanings. For example, the level of recognition and support accorded to an illness might differ depending how it is thought to have originated, the populations most affected by it, as well as how well known it is within our society. Often, a diagnosis of cancer elicits responses of sympathy, offers of support, or worry, concern, and fear. In contrast, individuals with chronic fatigue syndrome (CFS) can sometimes be faced with disbelief or questioning over the validity of their illness.

The language used when describing different illnesses can also vary markedly. With a cancer diagnosis, the language used tends to externalise the condition. For example, clinicians, friends, and family might refer to the person as being unlucky to have Cancer come along, indicating that there was nothing a person could have done to prevent the diagnosis. With a cancer diagnosis, there are also frequently physical changes in the body that are visible to the eye or on scans, and which can be comprehended more successfully by a modernist/structuralist framework. People receive a specific diagnosis and treatment plan, and may be offered surgery or targeted therapies such as radiotherapy, chemotherapy, or biological therapies. With CFS, the cause of the condition is relatively unknown and not observable (by the same means). Therefore, a sense of questioning can occur as to whether or not a person has an illness. The language used can also, at times, situate the CFS illness experience as being within the control of the individual, with comments such as the person must have been "overdoing it" or is "just tired and lazy". This narrative can prove unhelpful, and CFS patients have often found themselves "fighting" to get a diagnosis, as they do not feel believed.

Weingarten (2001) described how she began to notice that people frequently constructed personal stories in keeping with broader themes; broader themes that are less visible, or less supported, in consultations within health settings. She referred to these broader themes as illness narratives, and went on to describe three that she considered particularly relevant (although she noted that there were likely many more):

> - Narratives that speak of how familiar we are with a person's illness experience: the degree of cultural resonance.
> - Narratives that speak of the course of a person's illness: whether it is considered stable, progressing (improving), or regressing (worsening).
> - Narratives that speak of the meaning made by the person themselves, or others, of the illness and the illness experience.

To give some examples, within our society cancer would be considered to have a high degree of cultural resonance. This can be helpful in that a person with cancer may not feel that they have to do as much explaining about the condition to others. Yet at other times, having such a "high profile" might mean that other people feel that they understand more about an affected person's experience than they do, or that a person is subject to lots more ideas about how they should be coping with this illness.

In contrast, many individuals with a diagnosis of HIV have said that living with HIV was not their main problem, but rather the fear that people would find out about their diagnosis. This fear sometimes had the effect that people delayed taking their medication, or chose not to take it at all. People could also take steps to isolate themselves or step back from possible relationships or sexual encounters in response to this fear. This is another example where cultural resonance may be prominent—but an illness being "well known" does not always equal increased support or understanding. This may be due to dominant ideas about perceived "fault", for example, about the way a person may have contracted the virus, or judgements about lifestyle. Sexually contracted conditions appear particularly vulnerable to negative value judgements.

The second illness narrative taps into Weingarten's reflections that some descriptions of illness appear both easier to talk about as well as easier to be heard by others. Frequently, the conversation hoped for in a clinic situation is one where the person comes to clinic to say that the treatment is working and that there is a reduction in symptoms. Yet how easy is it for a clinician to hear that a person does not feel that they are improving, or worse still, are deteriorating? And what if such reports continue over time? What effect might this have on medical team/patient interactions, in the face of not fitting with the dominant narrative of cure and improvement?

The third illness narrative is one that relates to the illness experience itself, and Weingarten made reference to three sub-experiences that she frequently came across within this theme. The first: the restitution narrative refers to the view that if you take your tablets and adhere to the advice from the team, you will be okay. And if something does happen, then all that can be done will have been done. This narrative is common and can also feel easier to hear but, for many, this does not fit with their experiences, all or some of the time.

> One person I met with often talked about the despair he felt in relation to his diagnosis three years on. He found it difficult to make sense of these feelings and found himself especially troubled by the length of time since diagnosis, as he believed he should have "accepted this by now and be getting on with it".

These types of feelings can be harder to voice but also harder to listen to. Sometimes a person will find themselves unable to put their experience into words, or any form of coherent story. Weingarten refers to this as the chaos narrative, which is the second of her sub-narratives. The third is the quest narrative (Frank, 1995). This narrative describes new meanings made as a result of living with an illness. For example, some people may report that becoming unwell has been a good thing for them, as it has meant that they had to slow down and re-evaluate what is important for them in their life. They have then been able to take actions that focus on those aspects of life to which they give particular value. Weingarten's narratives, alongside some of the wider discourses mentioned, can be helpful in that they provide entry points for therapists to discussions about a person's own (specific) personal illness narratives:

> The importance above all else [being] to bear witness to the stories people tell when affected by physical illness, to tolerate these stories, to honour them, and to try to help people make some kind of sense of them.
>
> (Whittaker, 2009, p. 50)

Why are discourses of illness so important?

The central point is that meanings developed more broadly within society not only shape understandings and responses from a societal level, but also personal experiences and choices. They have the potential, therefore, to influence decisions made about treatment options, strategies used to cope with health conditions, alongside how a person may choose to make sense of any diagnoses. Predominately, they do this by developing particular ideas or "prescriptions" about how a person should be, or more specifically how they should be in relation to their health. We like to refer to these as "oughts" and "shoulds", and these can include ideas such as:

You should "battle" cancer.
You should "milk" every day and "live it" as if it is your last.
You should "spiritually grow" from your experience of living with an illness.

Of course, such ideas are not wrong and, in many cases, dominant ideas can feel helpful for a person.

For example, while undertaking training, one of the authors was diagnosed with dyslexia. At that time, in part, the label proved useful. It helped with understanding that rather than being "stupid", she learned in different ways. Clearly, this particular explanation or storying of the difficulties was useful and helpful, and a "good fit" with expectations within a structure.

However, there may also be times when labels and narratives feel unhelpful, and do not fit well with what an individual wants and hopes for their life. For example, individuals within the cancer service frequently said the following:

"I know I should be grateful that I've survived."
"I thought I would feel different/better about myself if I got through this."
"Everyone is telling me that I look great, but inside I feel awful."
"My friends and family are telling me I can fight this, but what if I can't, what if I don't want to, what does that say about me?"

These sayings clearly highlight a gap between how individuals saw themselves, and how they interpreted or perceived others to view how they should be living with their illness. Many of these comments were likely prompted by discourses communicated by media, friends, and professionals:

> You're still here, so you should be happy and making the most of your life.
> You should fight cancer, rather than give up.
> It's a life-changing experience, and you can grow from it.

As therapists, it feels important, therefore, to remain alert to when generalised ideas may not be working for a person, as this disconnect has the potential to leave a person vulnerable to feelings of self-blame, failure, helplessness, or even doubting their worth as a person. "Illness or, more accurately, our relationship to it, threatens the way we know ourselves and how others know us also" (Weingarten, 2001, p. 2). While not "wrong", these ideas might simply not be the right story for that person's experience. It is interesting to reflect on just how influential dominant discourse can be for a person. How often, though, do such discourses remain unnoticed or uncommented on during therapeutic work with people? And while it is impossible for therapists to completely step outside of dominant discourses, they surround each and every person, and all would be lost without them. Narrative perspectives believe that by making these ideas visible to a person, it does become possible to explore them. This increased awareness allows for a person to evaluate what they would like to hold on to in their lives, in addition to what they would prefer to have less prominent within their lived experience. Thus, narrative conversations can provide opportunities to explore storying that fits better for a person, and is more in line with what they give value to.

On one final but important point, the issue of oughts and shoulds becomes particularly relevant when we consider behaviours referred to as "non-adherence" or "non-compliance". By deconstructing expectations potentially held by a person and team, and exploring what fits better for the person, we can often make progress in shifting perceived "stuck" situations around compliance.

Part two: ideas for ways to bring conversations about discourse into your work with people

Deconstruction

The practice referred to as "deconstruction" is an incredibly useful tool when it comes to bringing these ideas into the therapeutic space. Indeed, we would argue that everything that we will now discuss is a form of deconstruction, or a description of tools that can be used to support it. Michael White referred to deconstruction as "practices which reveal the hidden assumptions behind these taken for granted truths; and which reveal who benefits and who loses from these assumptions" (Walther, Redstone, & Fox, 2013, p. 2). Concepts are the cultural means by which information is brought together, and their differences and similarities discerned. They are important in that they help create shared understandings and tend to reflect ideas agreed upon by a number of people, over a period of time. Some will go on to reach the status of "common sense" and, once achieved, it will usually be taken for granted that they exist or represent a truth in some way.

Having been heavily influenced by social constructionist ideas, narrative therapists tend to be very interested in concepts. It is not that they consider them "bad" in any way, indeed it is recognised that they provide us with the short-hand required for communication. But rather, narrative therapists hold the view that concepts will always reflect generalisations, and use of them without any form of deconstruction will assume meaning while missing the detail (Walther & Carey, 2009). Moreover, rather than being a mere description of life, as with all language, narrative therapists view concepts as formative. Thus expectations about ways we should be (or live our lives) are inherent within them. Within physical health, you will have likely heard several concepts stated as if they were something of which everyone is aware, is signed up to, or subject to. Consider "adjustment problems", or even just the idea of "adjustment", "compliance", and "stages of grieving". Spending time unpacking ideas like these can be really helpful. It can open up conversations, develop richer descriptions, and expand difference.

On the latter point, concepts are often thought of as if they exist as just one entity, for example, "love", "caring", or "adjustment" can all be seen to reflect one type of thing. Yet a person may consider there to be many different forms of love, many different expressions of caring, or many different actions that come under the umbrella of adjustment (Walther & Carey, 2009). The process of deconstruction can support a person to become clearer about what may be similar or different within each understanding. It allows for more stories to be available to a person and can support a person to think about how they might like to position themselves in relation to these ideas.

Some ideas for questions to support deconstruction:

Can you tell me a little more about this word (i.e., "adjustment")?
Where did you first hear it? What are your thoughts about what it relates to?
How would you know if you were "adjusting" or "adjusting well"?
Who else might hear/know about this concept? How long do you think it has been around? What other ideas do you think feed into it/relate to it/ are influenced by it?
What ideas do you think the team have in relation to "adjusting well", what would they hope you would be doing/not be doing/doing less of/doing more of?
Are these ideas that fit with you? Do any of these ideas/actions feel important (or more important) to you?
What difference would it make if you were doing more/less of this, or if you were giving less weight to this concept?
What skills/knowledge might be required to do more of this? What might you have to draw on, keep hold of, or think about? Where has this understanding of how to do this come from? How did these skills develop?

Alternatively, the therapist may wish to simply "unpack" what people mean when they refer to particular conditions, terms, or statements. Writing down whatever thoughts, images, feelings, or judgements occur about a particular illness or health term can be a useful exercise to begin the process of deconstruction of a concept. For example, with reference to Macmillan:

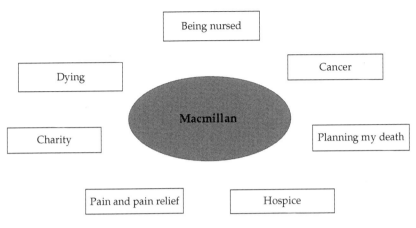

Figure 3.1. An example of a visual way to deconstruct a concept.

Talking to Macmillan nurses, the words that a person might choose to describe their roles could include:

- laughter
- support
- recovery
- listening
- standing by people
- sharing the pain
- thinking in steps
- hearing people's wishes

It may also be the case that people use the "same" words, but have different concepts of the *meaning* of that word when applied to a particular context. The process of thinking together in this way can open up possibilities by putting forward the idea that concepts are not fixed in their meaning nor neutral. These are points that can then be built upon.

Using maps to support the process of deconstruction

Narrative maps of practice are especially helpful to conversations that aim to deconstruct dominant discourses of illnesses. Within this chapter, we would like to explore two that appear well suited to the task. These are the Statement of Position Map One and the Context and Discourse Map.

Statement of Position Map One (SOPM1)

This map has been discussed at some length within the problem exploration chapter, but we would like to take a moment to highlight how it can be used with the deconstruction of discourses.

> Mary talked about being a mother of a child with a neurological disorder and working with her child's school. She talked about not wanting to be "one of those mothers". This was with reference to being the mother of a poorly child, and the ideas that she and others held about those mothers in the context of their relationships with schools.

Starting with the first category of SOPM1 (identify the problem), the worker can characterise and richly describe the idea of being "one of those mothers" by asking questions such as "How would you know if a teacher was viewing you as one of those mothers?"; "How does one of those mothers act and think?" And even moving on to naming the problem (dominant social discourse): "Following on from what you have told me, what name would you give for this kind of behaviour, or way of being?"

The therapist can also use category two of SOPM1 (exploring the effects) to ask about the effects of this discourse. For example, "When people view you as being 'one of those mothers', how does it have you acting?", and "How does it affect your relationship with the teachers and the school?"; "Are there times when you notice this feeling of being seen as 'one of those mothers' as particularly strong?"

The therapist could then ask Mary to evaluate these effects with the intention of encouraging her to take a position on them. They could do this by asking if the effects fit with what Mary wants for her life, and then ask "In what way?". The conversation could then move on to ask whether the discourse of being "one of those mothers" was blocking, obstructing, or detracting from what Mary gave value to in any way. In response to this, Mary might talk about how saddened she was that she was not able to work as collaboratively with the school as she wished. Mary might have hopes to become an integral part of the school community, in a mutually supportive and friendly relationship. Perhaps in a joint endeavour of working with the school to give her son an enjoyable and stimulating time in his primary school years.

The Context and Discourse Map

The Context and Discourse Map, often referred to as the Shoulds to Coulds Map, was developed by Walther, Redstone, and Holmgren (2014). It is a two-part map that encourages people to first consider how problems are developed in context, and the discourses that may potentially contribute to them. The map then moves on to exploring and evaluating the effects of any identified discourse, as well as discussing possibilities for living that are potentially better suited to the person in question and their values.

> **Part 1 of the map: basing the difficulties in the context of social norms ...**
> How do these difficulties affect you? Who else do you think they may affect?
> What ideas (norms or expectations) may be behind or inform these difficulties?
> Where do you think these ideas come from?
> Who do these ideas support, and who do they undermine?
>
> **Part 2 of the map: exploring how the discourse affects the person, and what they give value to ...**
> What do these norms or expectations tell you about how you ought or should be?
> What do these oughts have you doing to "change" yourself?
> What effects are they having on your relationships and how you view yourself?
> Are there times when you can't be bothered with these oughts, or just flat refused to listen to them?
> What does this refusal to follow or listen to these ideas make possible for you?
> How would you describe this act of refusal? What name would you give to it?
> If you were able to continue to refuse these ideas more often, what might be possible for you, what options would it make more available to you?

Mary spoke of a time when her son's wheelchair had been turned over during a playground incident, and her son's arm had been bruised. The next school day, Mary brought her son to school as usual and warmly greeted the teaching staff on playground duty. She remembered some of the staff seeming surprised at this, and slightly wary. When she spoke to the assistant headteacher at the end of the day, it was admitted to her that many of the staff had been expecting her to not bring her son in that day, and perhaps to make angry phone calls to the headteacher. Mary said how she had smiled at the assistant head and simply said that all children had accidents, and that she appreciated how her son had been allowed by the school staff to get in the thick of playing with his friends. And that her son was not unduly hurt, and had laughed about how much fun he had had that day. This seemed to be a turning point in Mary's relationship with the school. Later, Mary spoke about her relief about the school "finally being able to really see what kind of parent I am".

Use of metaphors

Conversations about discourse can be at risk of becoming too wordy, too distant from a person's experience, or full of jargon. Using metaphors developed by the person can be especially helpful in avoiding this. The therapist can encourage individuals to use metaphors to help explain how they are feeling.

I have frequently heard how people can feel as though they are stuck at the bottom of a dark well or pit, and unable to climb out, in response to living with an illness. If a person describes their mood in relation to their illness as often like as if they are trapped in a deep, dark well, then I might then be able to explore further by drawing on their metaphor, for example, by asking:

Further questions can be asked about the metaphor to deepen understanding:

Does it feel okay for me to ask you about The Well again?
Where are you in relation to it now?

By using people's words, images, understandings—in essence, their personally constructed stories—we can also follow how people's analogies or metaphors may change. For example, they may find themselves:

Sinking further into The Well?

Or they can relate their position in relation to the problem:

Only see a glimmer of light at the top of The Well.

Metaphors also provide us with opportunities to hear about how people may have faced the problem and found a way to deal with it, for example:

What has helped you climb nearer to the top of The Well, since you slipped down further last week?

Valuing the expertise of the individual

Dominant discourses can imply that others (other than the person themselves) are in possession of the knowledge, skills, and expertise to understand and manage an illness. One of the central tasks of narrative therapists is to ensure that a person's expertise, knowledge, and skills in understanding and telling their lived experience are privileged. The therapist is acting merely as facilitator of this process—neither the expert nor the author of the storying:

As a newly qualified therapist working in a cancer service, I was apprehensive that I did not have a vast knowledge or understanding of cancer, symptoms, or treatments. Yet the individual sat in front of me will likely come with so much more medical knowledge, having attended many appointments and potentially lived with the symptoms for a long time. As time went on, I learned more about the types of cancers, the treatment options, and became more aware of likely symptoms, however, this did not change the fact that the patient was the expert in their experience of living with this illness.

The worker must learn as much as possible about the person's understanding and knowledge of their condition, ways of coping, and what they give value to.

I began working with a young man with a diagnosis of leukaemia, who asked for psychological support as he felt he "wasn't coping". He said that he did not feel able to contain his emotions. We spent a lot of time discussing his cancer journey. This allowed us to step into his storying, and from this viewpoint, spot intentions, unique outcomes, values, and principles. He discussed how he gave value to relating to other people, this had helped him to develop relationships with the staff and fellow patients on the ward. The camaraderie of the ward and his humour helped him to cope, and he learned that this had helped others too, which in turn made him feel as though he had a purpose. At first, he spoke about how he set timescales and goals, but then quickly explained how he had learned that he needed to drop these timescales, as they frequently led him to feel disappointed.

The above example highlights how adept and skilful individuals can be in finding ways to help themselves cope. Therapists working within these settings can at times feel overwhelmed by conversations about illness, death, and dying. However, it is conversations such as the one illustrated above that can also lead the worker to feel inspired to look beneath the surface of dominant discourses around a person, and thus hear amazing and uniquely personal stories of coping.

A note about language

Exploring language and words used is frequently the medium most readily applied within therapy, but storying can equally occur through observations of art, play, or of other mediums. For example, when an individual undergoing chemotherapy arrives for a review appointment without their wig on for the first time, we might ask what this means for them and what may have led them to take this action. Moreover, as in the example above, a therapist can collaboratively re-author a person's illness journey by highlighting the steps taken to reduce the effects of the problem on his life, both using a traditional written format as well as through the use of pictures, charts, and videos.

A note about the system

In addition to individual discussions with a person, it is helpful to extend conversations to a person's family or medical team. It is possible that the people surrounding a person may have different ideas about how to live with an illness, which (potentially) might be playing a central role in maintaining the presence of oughts or shoulds. The therapist can use the ideas described with the relevant people, or medical teams, as a means of deconstructing dominant discourses and opening space for lesser-told ways of living and coping to be heard and acknowledged. Sometimes just sharing stories from experience and published research can begin to "loosen" ideas or suggest alternative stories/ explanations. An example of this concerns the construct of happiness, which is more complex than we may at first consider. In Diener, Suh, Lucas, and Smith's (1999) study, they found that self-reported perceptions of happiness correlated significantly with self-rated perceptions of good health. In contrast, the physician's contemporaneous ratings of that person's health did not correlate with ratings of the person's happiness and perceptions of life quality. This reminds practitioners to not be overly reliant on "objective" measures in lieu of bringing forth the person's lived experience. For more discussion on working with systems, please read the chapters on re-authoring, in-patient, and indirect working.

In conclusion

The principal intention behind this chapter has been to introduce you, as the reader, to several of the key ideas and philosophies that underpin the narrative approach. We consider this to be important, as inevitably these broader ideas will trickle down to the personal narrative. Indeed, one way in which distress can be conceptualised (from a narrative therapy perspective) is in terms of an apparent mismatch or disconnect between what a person feels they are or should be doing, and what others or more generally society expects. By raising our awareness of the nature of discourse, and the revelation that these are simply ideas and possibilities, the therapist opens up space for the person to revise their relationship with them. Through our own experience, people have commented on the process of deconstruction and how freeing it can feel. The deliberate and conscious action to assume a particular position can reconnect a person with agency, and the belief that they can choose to do something different within their life. Thus facilitating the person to prioritise, privilege, and make visible one understanding over another, with consequent preferred effects upon how they live in relation to their illness.

Acknowledgements

To Stephen Weatherhead for the gentle push he gave me to grasp hold of this opportunity. I would like to thank my mum, sister, and Christian, for providing me with the support and reassurance that I could do it. And of course, thanks to Lincoln for his calmness and guidance in writing this chapter together. JP

To my brothers, sisters, father, and mother who always hoped and believed I would do this. Of course, my family, Jennifer Pomfret for generating such a wealth of interesting work, and Louise Mozo-Dutton who pulled this chapter from the ashes. And finally, thanks to Bruce Law for his feedback on this chapter. LS

References

Berger, P. L., & Luckmann, T. (1966). *The Social Construction of Reality: A Treatise in the Sociology of Knowledge*, Garden City, NY: Anchor Books.

Bruner, J. (1990). *Acts of Meaning.* Cambridge, MA: Harvard University Press.

Burr, V. (1995). *An Introduction to Social Constructionism.* London: Routledge.

Carey, M., & Russell, S. (2004). *Externalising Commonly Asked Questions: Narrative Therapy, Responding to Your Questions.* Adelaide: Dulwich Centre Publications.

Conrad, P., & Barker, K. K. (2010). The social construction of illness: key insights and policy implications. *Journal of Health and Social Behavior, 51*: 67–79.

Diener, E., Suh, E. M., Lucas, R. E., & Smith, H. L. (1999). Subjective well-being: three decades of progress. *Psychological Bulletin, 125*: 276–302.

Foucault, M. (1980). Two lectures. In: C. Gordon (Ed.), *Power/Knowledge: Selected Interviews and Other Writings* (pp. 1972–1977). Hemel Hempstead: Harvester Wheatsheaf.

Fox, N. J. (1993). Discourse, organisation and the surgical ward round. *Sociology of Health & Illness, 15*: 16–42.

Frank, A. (1995). *The Wounded Storyteller: Body, Illness and Ethics.* Chicago: University of Chicago Press.

Freud, S. (1896). The aetiology of hysteria. In: J. Strachey (Ed. and Trans.). *The Standard Edition of the Complete Psychological Works of Sigmund Freud, 3*: 189–224. London: Hogarth Press.

Gee, J. P. (1991). Memory and myth: a perspective on narrative. In: A. McCabe & C. Peterson (Eds.), *Developing Narrative Structure* (pp. 1–25). Hillsdale, NJ: Lawrence Erlbaum Associates.

Kierans, C. M., & Maynooth, N. U. I. (2001). Sensory and narrative identity: the narration of illness process among chronic renal sufferers in Ireland. *Anthropology & Medicine, 8*: 237–253.

Langellier, K. M. (2001). Personal narrative. In: M. Jolly (Ed.), *Encyclopaedia of Life Writing: Autobiographical and Biographical Forms* (pp. 699–701). London: Dearborn.

Redstone, A., Fox, H., Gorney, C., & Ord, P. (2012). *Linking Lives, Working with Groups and Communities: Level 3 Module Notes*. London: The Institute of Narrative Therapy.

Squire, C. (2005). Reading narratives. *Group Analysis, 38*: 91–107.

Walther, S., Redstone, A., & Fox, H. (2013). *Social Context, Discourse and Power: Level 3 Module Notes*. London: The Institute of Narrative Therapy.

Walther, S., Redstone, A., & Holmgren, A. (2014). Exploring discourses of caring: Trish and the impossible agenda. In: S. Weatherhead & D. Todd (Eds.), *Narrative Approaches to Brain Injury* (pp. 101–142). London: Karnac.

Walther, S., & Carey, M. (2009). Narrative therapy, difference and possibility: inviting new becomings. *Context, 105*: 3–8.

Weingarten, K. (2001). Making sense of illness narratives: braiding theory, practice and the embodied life. http://dulwichcentre.com.au/articles-about-narrative-therapy/illness-narratives/ (accessed 28 March).

White, M. (2002). Addressing personal failure. *The International Journal of Narrative Therapy and Community Work, 3*: 33–76.

White, M. (2007). *Maps of Narrative Practice*. New York: W. W. Norton.

White, M., & Epston, D. (1989). *Literate Means to Therapeutic Ends*. Adelaide: Dulwich Centre Publications.

Whittaker, R. (2009). Narrative explorations in clinical health psychology. *The International Journal of Narrative Therapy and Community Work, 2*: 48–58.

CHAPTER FOUR

Facilitating preferred change for children and young people

Lincoln Simmonds

This chapter is not a comprehensive review of narrative ideas in relation to physical health problems. Instead, the chapter complements other chapters by specifically examining principles of narrative therapy practice that have to be given particular emphasis when working with children and young people as opposed to adults. These principles can then assist in the application of the practice ideas discussed throughout this book.

Referral letters can at times promote the view that the problem is solely internalised within a young person or their family. This can have the effect of distributing a story that the person is in some way failing or lacking, or actively resisting the "right" course of action. Sometimes the problem story can be one that particularly diminishes the young person's agency, or elevates it to levels that do not pay heed to the relational and systemic aspects that may be coming into play. Such stories can be promoted to the extent that they obscure other alternative stories about young people. They can also make it harder for professionals to recognise opportunities to view the young person (or family) as an actor who is responding to relational and contextually bound difficulties.

Children and young people live within systems of family or within some form of care, education, a community, or even online. Young people often occupy positions of diminished power within these systems, as opposed to their adult counterparts. Thus, they may lack the opportunities to wield power and autonomy over their own lives, and influence those of others. This chapter discusses how a narrative therapist can work to facilitate the re-positioning of others to privilege the centring of the young person. This repositioning would be with the intention of developing and thickening preferred stories centred on the young person's hopes, dreams, and aspirations. The narrative therapist's intentions are to make a young person's preferred stories of their life more visible to themselves and others, and to also encourage a context more sustaining of them.

Laying the foundation

The following paragraphs discuss how to establish a context in which a young person's voice and expressions of preferred ways of living can be heard, acknowledged, supported, and acted on. The overarching aim of the therapist is to explore alternative preferred stories, when the dominant (problematic) account does not fit or support agency for the young person.

Positioning

It is often helpful to talk with parents/carers prior to the appointment. This conversation will usually acknowledge that they are bringing concerns about the young person, and that these concerns will be heard and thought about. However, such a pre-appointment conversation can also request their patience and commitment to allowing time for the young person to begin storying aspects of their lives. The example below is a dialogue that might typically take place with a parent/carer in preparation for an appointment.

> THERAPIST: I know that you had especially asked your GP if Sean could see a psychologist, so I imagine that there were a lot of things that you wanted to discuss with me. I wondered if it would be OK with you, though, if I could start the appointment by asking Sean some questions about his life in general. That might be talking about the problems, or it may be about talking about other things ...

FATHER: Things like what?

THERAPIST: Friendships, what he likes to do in his free time, who he feels close to, what hopes he has for his life.

FATHER: What? Why? We came to talk about his behaviour.

THERAPIST: Yeah, I know, and that's definitely something we will talk about, but I want to know a lot more about Sean than just The Behaviour … to …. well … in order to understand more about what is important to Sean, to find out how he wants to live his life.

FATHER: I don't know, it's difficult to understand what's going on inside his head. I just want him to be happy.

THERAPIST: If you did understand what was going on for him more, what difference might that make?

FATHER: Well, I guess then I could help him more …

As discussed, narrative therapy often involves working hard (right from the outset), to provide space for a young person's voice to be heard and expressed without chastisement or overt judgement. This often involves the facilitation of other participants placing themselves in a listening position. Parents or carers sometimes find it difficult and frustrating when the therapist focuses on the young person when they have come to share and discusses problems. To that end, stating this within the appointment letter can be helpful:

I find it very helpful to give the young person a chance to speak earlier on. Often, it is helpful to engage the young person in conversation about other areas of their life (seemingly) in exception to the problem they have come to talk about. Such information can often be very helpful in understanding what skills the young person has, and what they know about, and may also give us ideas about what the young person sees as important and how they would prefer to live their life. I understand that there are difficulties, and I will be allowing you time to talk about them, explore, and understand them. We can also think about ways of working with you to help reduce or manage the problem later on in the appointment.

The therapist is asking for permission to primarily have the conversations with the young person as opposed to the parents or carers, but may also seek permission to politely interrupt and "headline" conversations. This can have the effect of drawing people back to the conversational content and ensuring it remains centred on the young person. So, for example, a therapist might say to parents that she/he is particularly interested in finding out about a young person's hobbies and interests. The therapist would also be seeking information from parents/carers that may more richly describe the skills and knowledges that the young person draws on in engaging in the hobby or interest. The therapist can then work at developing preferred stories or unique outcomes which more richly describe the storying of that interest, and insights into what the young person gives value to in relation to the interest.

Questions that can be useful in this context can be drawn from work on definitional ceremonies and reflecting teams, in particular the outsider witness scaffold (see White, 1995 for more detail). The outsider witness scaffold is an especially helpful way of eliciting particular responses from those who have been listening to the conversation. Usually after the therapist and young person have spoken, the therapist will then ask parents/carers questions along the four categories of the outsider witness scaffold.

Questions about the listener's (parent's) responses to what they heard:
What were you particularly drawn to? What caught your interest?
Questions that attempt to help the listener identify what the young person gives value to in this context:
What does this suggest about [the young person]? What does it suggest to you about them, and what's important to them?
Questions that seek to establish a connection between the listener and the young person through resonance:
How did this resonate or remind you in some way of your own life and experiences?
Questions that look at how the conversation has affected the listener:
Where does this leave you? Having listened to this conversation and thought about it some more, has it taken you somewhere? Do you think this might lead you to do something more, or less, or differently in your life?

When using the outsider witness scaffold, it is important to keep the listener focused on what the young person actually said; thus, staying focused on what the words mean to that young person as opposed to being drawn into conversations centred more on the parent's views, wishes, and agendas.

The role of externalising

Externalising is a therapeutic tool, which has been discussed in earlier chapters of this text, and the reader can also refer to White (2007) for further information. Externalising conversations often have the effect of helping families/systems focus on working together to lessen the influence of the problem. This would be in contrast to the system viewing the problem as internal to the young person. It is important to pay heed to the "politics" of externalising, though: a therapist cannot simply decide to externalise anything without the editorial control of the young person at the centre of the work. The problem to be externalised must be from the perspective of the problem as viewed by the young person. The young person would ideally name the problem, a naming that would provide a view of the problem as something that they too are in a relationship with, and one that illustrates the diminishing effects of the problem on their preferred ways of living (as opposed to just the view of their parents, carers, or others).

> The therapist asked the parents and their seven-year-old son Gary if they had a name for the difficult behaviour that was arising within the family home. The parents immediately begin describing how they would say that "Larry" was in the room, when Gary was having a tantrum. The parents shared laughter, and as they spoke even more enthusiastically, relating tales about Larry, Gary seemed to physically shrink and become quieter.

Of course, there are times when we would work separately with parents and carers in order to explore and understand their concerns. This can provide opportunities for parents to develop their own preferred stories, which are often linked to the problem story and the young person's preferred accounts. When an appropriate externalised name is negotiated among family members, it is often the case that a common theme arises and the problem is found to be causing negative effects upon the lives and relationships of "all" members of the family. This externalising has the effect of centring the family on preferred alternative stories, which may have been obscured by the problem story. It can also reduce feelings of blame directed toward the young person, while emphasising that the young person (as well as parents and carers) has agency in ameliorating the effects of the problem.

> Lisa talked about the Angry Mutterings and how they would often come out after a difficult day at school. Her parents listened with interest as Lisa said that the Angry Mutterings helped her blow out steam at the end of the school day, but they could also lead her to say things that she regretted, leading to arguments in the house and Lisa sitting upstairs in her room feeling miserable. Lisa's parents began to talk about how they felt that the Angry Mutterings had kept all this information from them, they had thought that Lisa just didn't want to be around them, and they hadn't realised that the Angry Mutterings were around because of stresses at school. These Angry Mutterings had caused a lot of Misunderstandings in the family! We began to talk about whether there were other ways to help Lisa with the school stresses, ways that meant that she wasn't left isolated in her room, or that led to more Misunderstandings between Lisa and her parents.

* * *

Scaffolding

Scaffolding refers to a term first coined by Wood, Bruner, and Ross (1976), and which became synonymous with the work of the Russian psychologist Vygotsky. Scaffolding relates to how the narrative therapist works to keep the conversation within the person's range of lived experience and comprehension. Scaffolding in narrative therapy is defined as: the idea of making a scaffold of questions to help people move from what is "known and familiar" to "what is possible to know".

We can scaffold in terms of the words and phrases used in our questions, so that the language is accessible and shared with the person. We can scaffold via other mediums such as through play or drawing, or charting problematic or preferred stories. We can also spend time with young people, watching and listening to what they do, and then test out whether what we experienced of them (I have deliberately not used the word "observations", which speaks more of hypothesising and objectification) resonates with the young person or their carers in terms of preferred identity conclusions, skills, qualities, and knowledges. We can also use outsider witness practices in order to develop preferred stories.

George, a three-year-old boy, and the therapist have been engaged in sand and water play for half an hour. Nearer the end of the session, the therapist explores whether any preferred stories can be developed from the parent's observations of the play.

THERAPIST
[TURNS TO PARENT]:   So you were watching as George and I played with the water and sand ... what did you notice?

PARENT: He kept filling up the sand tray with water!

THERAPIST: Yes, he did, I was wondering at one time if he might spill it.

PARENT: Oh no, he didn't at all. George is very careful.

THERAPIST: Careful? Could you tell me about other times when you have noticed how careful George can be? Maybe careful in relation to things? Or it could be careful in relation to people?

Scaffolding with our language

Michael White's early writings were accused at times of being quite dense and impenetrable in terms of the language used. People would often say that they had to read paragraphs over and over again. It would be more accurate to say that he was very careful with language. Narrative therapists strive to be careful with language. This does mean at times that the therapy can be prone to asking questions that sound quite complex, or overly long. Finding ways to simplify questions is crucial in our work with young people. For example, "What do you give value to?" is a careful way of asking about what specifically is important to a young person, as opposed to general constructs of what is probably important to a young person. At times when young people are asked this question, they might say something like the environment is important to them, but how many of them would be following the Green Peace website or haranguing their parents to recycle more? Giving value to something is about particularly identifying a value that is specific to that person and their preferred ways of living. Such questions often lead to conversations about unique outcomes consistent with what is given value to. Such a question, though, could be simplified by asking:

> "OK, so you told me that looking after the environment is really important to you. Could you tell me a bit more about what this means to you day-to-day? Are there particular things that you do, or think about, at school or home concerning the environment? What is most important to you and your life, when you think about looking after the environment?"

Thus, we scaffold the person to their "near experience" and the intricacies of their own, as opposed to a general, sense of living.

More on language and scaffolding distance

The term "scaffolding distance" is a useful one with relevance to thinking about language. Simply put, the scaffolding distance may be too big a gap for the young person to traverse when questions are too distant from their experience. Thus the therapist may not have worded a question in an "experience-near" way, so not in a way that is within the young person's sphere of influence. The questions asked need to relate to the young person's understanding of themselves, their relationships, and the world. When this happens, the therapist should do their best to use questions that fit better with the young person's realm of experience, as opposed to their own expectations of (or ideas about) what may be going on.

> I have some ideas from working with other young people affected by The Big D [i.e., depression], but for you, could you tell me how I would know if The Big D was less present in your life? In which bits of your life would you first notice that The Big D was around less?

Drawing and charting

In this section, I will talk about drawing and charting. I have taken drawing to be with reference to the young person's drawings, when prompted by the therapist, spontaneously drawn, or brought to appointments during the course of therapy. I will take charting to be a way of the therapist summarising or editorialising developing stories, authored by the young person, or as a collaborative piece of documentation produced by therapist and young person. It may be the case that the therapist wishes to deliberately chart the young person's stories in a particular way, but he/she would always tentatively check whether this was appropriate, as well as remain open to alternative renditions of the story (or stories).

Drawing

Young people often take a piece of paper and draw a picture whilst waiting for their appointment. Asking permission to view the picture, talking about it, and the skills and knowledges used to draw it, even the history of drawing such representations, presents a variety of entry points into alternative stories. They can also be extremely useful for enriching existing preferred alternative narratives. Here are some questions that can be used to enquire about a young person's drawing:

> **Is there a history to this?** The therapist could thus ask the young person, "How long has this been around? Where did it come from?"
>
> **Who would appreciate this drawing?** The therapist could ask, "Who would know most about what you're drawing?"
>
> **Who supported and encouraged these skills?** The therapist could ask, "Who did you learn these things from, who taught you?"
>
> **What skills and knowledges did the young person draw on when producing these works?** The therapist could ask "How did you manage to do this?"
>
> **What does this [e.g., act of giving] suggest about the young person?** The therapist could ask, "What does this say about you, what you think is important, how you like to be?"

Often, young people produce pictures and images that are re-tellings of problem stories. Externalising and deconstructing the problem story can lead to previously obscured preferred alternative stories, or a richer description of an externalised characterisation of the problem.

> Greg had drawn a black curled line in the bottom corner of his picture of The Habit Monster. When asked about this, he said that it was the HDMI lead for his games console, as he said that The Habit Monster seemed to be much more present when he was playing video games.

* * *

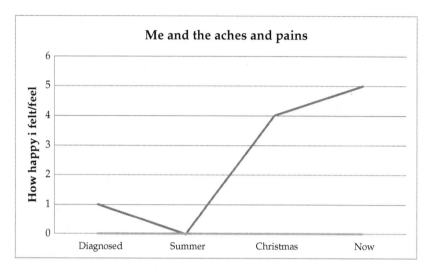

Figure 4.1. An example of charting.

Charting

The therapist can help a young person construct a chart or diagram to track the influence of the problem in their life. The chart below shows a graph with events occurring over time on the x-axis, and an evaluation of the event (from really bad to really good) on the y-axis. By evaluating the events in relation to the problem, the young person is often able to discriminate between events consistent with the problem story and those considered exceptions to it. These events can then be explored using Statement of Position Maps One, Two (SOPM1/2) and remembering conversations. Thus, through charting, the therapist can help the young person begin to scaffold towards preferred identity stories. I am aware that other therapists have used pie charts or Venn diagrams to chart the relationship between problem and other aspects of a young person's life, or to take a position in terms of the problem's influence and how this may change over time.

Lily talked about how going back to school after her admission to hospital, and subsequent diagnosis of juvenile arthritis, had been a positive experience. I tracked how she felt over time, as above, but also used categories of questions from SOPM2, to explore how she felt happier on returning to school (a unique outcome). Lily described how it had been like "having my support team round me" (naming). Having her support team around her had meant that she had felt more understood by others, that her friends were "there for her" and encouraged her in "taking care of her health". This clearly had been a positive experience for Lily with positive effects, which spoke of Lily giving value to a sense of "you don't have to do difficult things by yourself".

Messages within clinics

Messages within clinics can be both explicitly and implicitly supportive of dominant discourses pertaining to what constitutes a "good patient".

I once was sat in a clinic for young people with cystic fibrosis (CF) as a trainee practitioner, and noticed looking around on the walls that there were newspaper articles about a young person with CF. This young person had completed remarkable athletic feats in order to raise money for a CF charity. I looked again at the same walls, and noticed another article about a young person who attended the same clinic achieving four of the highest grades that one can achieve at A-level. I was impressed, but at the same time saddened. I wondered if there was room on the walls for achievements, which perhaps in general terms people would not usually find as remarkable, but within the sphere of the young person's life and family were no less spectacular, as they may have reflected unique outcomes or preferred alternative accounts. Thus the walls could be a testimony to these achievements, as the accounts might be as influential and no less fantastic for the young people themselves.

If the young people and their families could have chosen what went onto the walls of the clinic, my prediction is that they would have also included achievements such as:

Donna swam her 25 metres today.
James got a gold star for helping tidy away the toys today.
Peter got to The Nether on Minecraft.
Louise platted her hair for the first time.
Richard has grown four inches since last summer.
Ella got her first tooth today.
Betty gave me a hug when I dropped a wine glass.
And Fred grew his first sunflower, and it was over a metre tall!

Thus, a wall that is a testament and celebration of our actual lives, as opposed to celebrations of achieving some transient social construct of success. For dominant social constructs of success also beget the ideas of failure; failure to measure up to whatever society says is successful. Success then becomes that which seems to "excel" our so-called "ordinary lives". Do such dominant discourses suggest that people living with a chronic illness must overcome the restrictions of their illness and do extraordinary things? Perhaps in order to make the most of their lives? And if they do not, does that then mean they have failed in some way? Who should be measuring this failure or success anyway? And what is it? It would be more meaningful to view success as to what degree someone is stepping into preferred narratives about themselves, and to what degree this is (or is not) okay with them. Perhaps this would allow professionals to reflect more on the process of something that someone works on over time.

Using metaphor

Metaphors can be used to richly describe a problem or alternative preferred story. The metaphor is ideally developed by the young person as opposed to the narrative therapist or parent/carer. In facilitating this, the therapist may offer the young person the opportunity to hear other metaphors. The therapist can then ask if any of the examples resonate with their own experience. Such metaphors may even be derived from testimony records, which will be discussed later in this chapter. However, it is always the young person who re-stories, or edits, the creation of the metaphor.

Metaphors are preferably derived from a young person's life experiences; a good starting point is to encourage a young person to richly describe a particular interest that they have. The therapist can then list the skills and knowledges they have been developing in relation to this interest over time. Often, it can be helpful to engage in "guided research", whereby the therapist encourages the young person to act as their guide and mentor, who is introducing them to this interest. The therapist can also co-research new knowledges about the area of interest with the young person.

> In working with one young person who had been struggling academically, the conversation moved to talk about a rock musician who the young person liked, and who had diabetes. Together, the therapist and young

person agreed that it might be interesting to find out more about the life of this musician within a session. They discovered that the artist had also struggled with diabetes, but had persevered and later went on to complete a master's degree. They looked at what had helped the rock artist manage in high school and college, who had supported him, and what had sustained him. In doing this, the young person was then able to think about whether any aspects of the rock musician's experience resonated with his own, and he began to more easily identify what he could draw on in continuing mainstream schooling.

* * *

Observing play and interactions

Michael White (2005) wrote a paper on working with three brothers who had suffered traumatic experiences. The brothers did not speak any English, and Michael did not speak their language. Through an interpreter, Michael offered observations about their play. Therapists can support the development of preferred narratives by observing a young person, and then offering their observations. This process can provide entry points to preferred accounts that, with the help of the child or a figure close to them, can be expanded. As always in using material derived from observations, the therapist has to be tentative in offering them, as well as open to relinquishing them if they do not fit with the young person's perspective.

The narrative therapist would also argue that therapeutic material should never be derived solely from an observed (potentially) dominant discourse of children's play and development. Therefore, it is important not to assume a position of judging the perceived "normality" or "abnormality" of play and interactions. Instead, the therapist would transfer autonomy (or editorial rights) to the young person, who is then able to reject or amend the observation, as well as feed back their evaluation of it. If the observation resonates with them, it can be developed into a re-telling. Such re-tellings can be scaffolded into what the young person gives value to and thickened into preferred identity stories. This simple and brief example highlights the importance of enabling the young person to story their own experience, even in the face of more dominant ideas about how a child behaves and reacts:

Judy, aged four, had grown up in a family that had been subject to years of domestic violence. Within a therapy play session, Judy picked up a doll and began bashing its head on the floor. The therapist, feeling concerned, asked Judy what she was doing. Judy looked up, and moved the doll so that the therapist could see a plastic figure halfway in and out of a tractor toy. "It's stuck", Judy replied, "I was banging it out".

Therapists often have to work hard to destabilise dominant narratives and discourses around the power of adults and the subjugation of children within the therapeutic context. Narrative therapists seek to allow the child to know that their views can differ from, and take precedence over, those of the therapist. Young people are encouraged to take the lead within the session and in developing their narrative. This is not the same as having an expectation that a young person will take the lead, and will be able to step into such a position easily, but rather that a therapist can support the young person in voicing their preferred ways of living. Narrative therapists will strive to do this in a way that does not inadvertently result in a young person feeling pressured, nor that they have to acquiesce or agree to the process.

Remembering practices

How often has it been the case that therapists meet with young people who have brought another virtual person or figure into the room? Perhaps it is someone they have seen in a film or TV programme, a cartoon, comic, or book character, or a friend, relative, or neighbour. The young person brings stories of this person or people, fictional or real, dead or alive, into therapeutic conversations. This raises the question of why they have chosen to do this? And what is their connection to this person? What is it about this figure or character that speaks of something that they give value to? Which aspects of this person's life resonate with their experience or hopes? Michael White spoke of re-membering conversations (White, 2000); conversations that help identify what a person gives value to through their relationship with another. White developed categories of questions to support exploration of this, and the reader can refer to White (2000) for more information.

There are, however, occasions when the characters brought into a room, or their relationship to them, is viewed as problematic or a feature of the dominant problem story. It might be that a character seems to encourage the young person to engage in acts of aggression and violence. Engaging in double listening is important here, as unique outcomes or preferred stories may still be identifiable. This process may also present opportunities for the young person to re-script their relationship to the characters that they have been drawn to.

Aaron, aged six years, was brought to see a therapist about his difficulties in having blood tests and his "anger issues"; throughout the first appointment, he kept talking about Optimus Prime. His mother said that she hated him "obsessing about Transformers", as it often meant that he enacted scenes of violence from the films. Aaron often referred to himself as Optimus. During the second appointment, the therapist asked Aaron to tell him everything he knew about Optimus Prime, and with his permission, they co-researched Optimus Prime with his mother during the session. During the course of the research, it became evident that Optimus Prime was a leader. Aaron's mother agreed that "being in charge" was important to Aaron. This then led to a conversation with Aaron and his mother about what he liked about being in charge, which led to a conversation about Aaron giving value to situations being predictable and understandable. This conversation moved to discussions with the medical team about the importance of Aaron being in charge, in relation to his blood tests. From there, a number of unique outcomes developed, including having the same staff member taking Aaron's blood, and Aaron choosing the site and method of taking the blood.

* * *

Outsider witness practices

Outsider witness practices, as described by White (1995, 2000), can be used for exploring and thickening preferred alternative accounts of a person. Outsider witnesses are an audience of people who can be drawn from family, friends, professionals, neighbours, or even people who have had experience of similar problems. This audience will then bear witness to a telling or re-telling of a person's experiences. The outsider witness scaffold (map) has been described fully in Walther and Fox (2012) and has four categories of enquiry:

- identifying the expression
- identifying the image
- identifying resonance
- identifying transport

Identifying the expression

This is focused on helping the outsider witness voice what they were particularly drawn to in the conversation between therapist and young person. It is important to encourage the outsider witness to focus on the actual words they heard spoken, as opposed to using their own words, which may speak of hypotheses about the young person. For example, "Whilst you were listening to this conversation, what did you hear that you were most drawn to?" (Walther & Fox, 2012).

If the outsider witness's response is one of stepping back into hypothesis by using words or ideas that were not present within the conversation, the therapist can gently draw them back to words said. Walther and Fox (2012) gave an example of an outsider witness stating, "I thought they were very brave" (which seemed to indicate a hypothesis *about* the young person); in response the therapist enquired "What did you actually *hear* that made you think that?" Specifically refocusing a person in this way can help reconnect them to the young person's actual expressions.

Identifying the image

In this stage, outsider witness responses can explored further by exploring what the expression suggests to them about the young person, and what they give value to: "As you listened to [the young person and therapist] talk about [the young person's] experiences, what did it suggest to you about what they might consider important? Do any particular pictures or images come to mind?"

Identifying the resonance

At this stage, we seek to connect the outsider witness to the young person's experiences: "Having listened to this conversation, and thought about it, is there anything that resonates or chimes with your own life or work? And if so, why and in what way?"

Identifying the transport

The fourth and final stage of the scaffold; Walther and Fox beautifully explain how this is a direct validation of how the young person's account has moved or affected the outsider witness. "It is rarely acknowledged that therapy is a two-way process and that not only is the person at the centre affected by the process, but those who are in the position of 'helper'" (Walther & Fox, 2012, p. 14). Thus the therapist might ask questions such as: "Having listened to this account, how has it affected you? Where has it left you or left you thinking? What might you take from this?"

Key to outsider witness practice is the careful preparation of all involved. Selection is important, as the therapist and young person are seeking people who can support the young person's preferred accounts. Those chosen need to be there for their role in bearing witness to a different type of conversation. Glenda Fredman (2014) has written extensively about this, and I would direct the reader to her paper for a more detailed account.

The therapist can seek permission from participants to interrupt the flow of conversation at times. This is in relation to the narrative therapist seeking responses that will support the preferred stories of the young person. Often, there will be a heading to the discussion, for example, "I particularly want to hear about John's music". Having a theme, and making this clearly known, can be a helpful means of focusing the outsider witnesses, and then, as the conversation progresses, a way of interrupting and re-focusing them if needed.

This practice can take many forms. It can be an indirect process of seeking feedback about a young person, or asking people to answer a questionnaire about them via letters or emails. More direct methods include face-to-face interviewing of the outsider witnesses with the young person present, or interviewing the young person in the presence of outsider witnesses, or both! Participants can be interviewed without the young person. However, the young person being there enables them to directly hear and contemporaneously respond to reflections as they are given. Participants will also bear witness to this, which can open up possibilities for the therapist to seek additional responses (from the young person) to what the participants have said, and lead to further opportunities to thicken preferred accounts.

Documents, testimonies, letters

It can be helpful to write narrative therapy letters within the session, actually co-written with the people to whom they are sent. The process of co-writing can explicitly underline a person's authorship in that they are the authors of the letter. Thus the narrative therapist is able to check how the letter fits with the person's experience, as well as provide opportunities for the person to write the letter themselves, or as much as they feel able to partake in the process. This provides a forum or context for the person to respond to what is being written in an editorial way. Thus emphasising the idea that the letter can be amended and used as the young person wishes, for example deciding with whom (if anyone) they would like to share it.

There are other documents as well as therapeutic letters that can be helpful here. Freedman, Epston, and Lobovits (1997, pp. 112–124, pp. 166–167), for example, illustrate how certificates can be used to mark and celebrate achievements consistent with preferred accounts of oneself. It can also be useful to include drawings and charts within documents, in order to further highlight what preferred accounts have been developed or identified in the course of appointments. For a more extended discussion on documenting practices, please see the final chapter in this book.

Rituals and celebrations

Rituals and celebrations can be powerful in signifying a unique outcome, commitment, or principle for living. They provide a context in which other aspects of life can be celebrated, in contrast to events and commitments derived from dominant narratives within Western society. They can also symbolise movement away from the influence of problem stories, and towards preferred alternative stories. Hence, celebrations invite an audience to bear witness to this testimony, and serve as a way of thickening and enriching preferred story developments. In narrative therapy, rituals are often done collaboratively with the young person, and are named in some way. An example of such a celebration might be how a family could ritualise a young person's transition to self-injecting for diabetes management:

Peter decided that Thursday 12th April was going to be "Injection Day". On this day, Dad had to return early from work so everyone in the family could be present. Peter would then inject himself listening to "Take That" in his bedroom on his own. When he came out from his room, smiling, the family were holding "Congratulations" banners, and Peter and his sister were then taken to Toys R Us for a treat.

Designing such rituals and celebrations ideally would involve the young person as the author or consultant. Thus, they would decide who would make up the audience, perhaps the words used or other mediums (such as "becoming a big girl"), then arrangement of the ritual/celebration itself, and what role each participant would play. Rituals can be perceived as an end in themselves, as one-off events, which mark a passage or transition. However, this is just one story in a myriad of possible stories about rituals, and they can also be ongoing and regular. The therapist might want to consider whether a particular ritual is in some way an expression of a preferred account of the young person. It can be the case that the young person's rituals are termed as obsessions or compulsions and viewed as problematic by professionals and/or family members. At those times, therapists can think about whether the young person views the rituals (or rather, their effects) as problematic, and whether they serve some benefit or preferred function for a young person. Narrative therapists may also wish to consider the absent but implicit with respect to these rituals, which might develop alternative stories consistent with what the young person gives value to.

For further reading around celebrations and rituals, see Freedman, Epston, and Lobovits (1997, pp. 140–142), where many excellent examples of practice have been documented.

In conclusion

Working with children and young people from a narrative perspective involves scaffolding problem exploration towards preferred story development, while considering how the positioning of the young person and others can facilitate this process. Often, the role of the therapist is not only to facilitate but at times directly reorganise the positioning of systems and people around a young person. This is in order to ensure that the work remains centred on the young person and their knowledge, skills, values, and hopes.

Acknowledgements

Many thanks to my family, and to my colleagues Hugh Fox for ideas and inspiration, Louise Mozo-Dutton (for picking me up and dusting me off over and over again), and Sarah Walther's encouragement, and for being an excellent role model. And finally to Ruth McIver for her feedback on this chapter.

References

Fredman, G. (2014). Weaving networks of hope into families, practitioners and communities: inspirations from systemic and narrative therapies. *Australian and New Zealand Journal of Family Therapy, 35*: 54–71.

Freedman, J., Epston, D., & Lobovits, D. (1997). *Playful Approaches to Serious Problems: Narrative Therapy with Children and Their Families*. New York: W. W. Norton.

Walther, S., & Fox, H. (2012). Narrative therapy and outsider witness practice: teachers as a community of acknowledgement. *Educational & Child Psychology, 29*: 10–19.

White, M. (1995). Reflecting teamwork as definitional ceremony. In: M. White (Ed.), *Re-Authoring Lives: Interviews and Essays* (pp. 1–17). Adelaide: Dulwich Centre Publications.

White, M. (2000). Reflecting team work as definitional ceremony revisited. In: M. White (Ed.), *Reflections on Narrative Practice: Essays and Interviews* (pp. 59–85). Adelaide: Dulwich Centre Publications.

White, M. (2005). Children, trauma and subordinate storyline development. *The International Journal of Narrative Therapy and Community Work, 3 & 4*: 10–21.

White, M. (2007). *Maps of Narrative Practice*. New York: W. W. Norton.

Wood, D., Bruner, J., & Ross, G. (1976). The role of tutoring in problem solving. *Journal of Child Psychology and Child Psychiatry, 17*: 89–100.

CHAPTER FIVE

Facilitating preferred change within in-patient settings

Louise Mozo-Dutton

When you are in hospital, every little thing matters, it doesn't matter what it is because you have nothing else, you are in hospital and that's all of your world.

So it matters about time taken to respond to a call bell. So it matters if people say they will see you at a certain time then turn up late. So it matters when people say that you are non-compliant but haven't helped you with your food.

Sometimes you can feel that you just exist, you don't feel like a person, you are just existing, a thing that needs medication. They can sometimes treat the body but not the person; it can leave you feeling worthless.

You are relying on people, so it is important that they take the time to listen and that they explain why they are doing something, the reasons for it, that they take the time to get to know you.

Quote from Gary, who spent over six months in hospital

As Gary's reflections highlight, the experience of being admitted to hospital can be an unsettling one, people can find themselves outside of their familiar environment, perhaps without their own clothes and sometimes away from loved ones. The person therefore becomes a "patient" and their life condensed to files at the end of their bed. As Gary notes, as patients, we have to rely on those around us to offer us the care and help that we need. This required reliance positions a person and their staff team in a particular way. Consequently, this chapter focuses largely on issues of power and agency: issues that, in my opinion, are central to this work.

So what can be different about in-patient work?

The theme of this book is on facilitating preferred change. Yet within the context of in-patient work, this often prompts the question of preferred change for whom?

In my experience, I have often been asked to meet with someone whom, I later discover, is unaware that they have been referred to psychology. My arrival can come as a shock, and has been met with anger or upset at times. Usually, though, I have noticed that it can be particularly difficult to say no. I am almost always able to locate a person, and thus the typical means of opting out by telephoning the department, ignoring letters, not attending appointments, or even not answering the door, are not available in hospital. It may only be after considerable discussion and reassurance that a person feels able to say this. Unlike in outpatient settings, therefore, I have found it harder to ensure that the usual prerequisites to seeing a therapist have been met, and that an informed choice has been made.

With healthcare staff being the predominate referrers, the reasons underlying a referral tend to be complex and require a degree of unpacking. This is largely due to the therapist being seen as an additional team member who can help move people through hospital. Indeed, business cases tend to be made on the basis that you "invest to save". Thus by commissioning psychology, counselling, or psychotherapy, it is anticipated that in-patient stays become shortened, repeat admissions reduced, and the hospital process smoothed. This raises the question of why it is that therapists are asked to meet with the people they do? Not everyone who enters hospital is requested to complete a mood screen, or invited to have a conversation with staff about how they feel. Indeed, given the considerable time and financial pressures on the system, there is usually limited room for discussion outside of why a person is in hospital, their current treatment, and how long before they can leave. So I began to wonder whether those referred are, in some way, viewed as not quite fitting with the standard care and treatment offered. And whether there was something about the hospital environment and the discourses that operate within it that relates to my initial reflection of "preferred change for whom?".

In addition to these areas of perceived difference, working within in-patient settings also means managing the practicalities of an environment generally less conducive to therapeutic conversations. Negotiating to talk with someone on an acute medical ward is no easy feat, and while some may be in a side room, which allows for more privacy, most people are nursed in bays with just a curtain separating them from others. Pulling a curtain around a bed can give the illusion of privacy but does not offer this. If a person is able to mobilise or be supported to transfer into a wheelchair, a therapist may find an unoccupied room. However, for some, moving out of bed is not an option, or they may require help from staff to do so which is not available at the time. There are also set meal times, visiting hours, and at various points a conversation may be interrupted for doctors' rounds, observations, bloods to be taken, and toilet breaks. Furthermore, a therapist must be mindful that a person may only tolerate talking for a short period of time, given how unwell or tired they feel. Working within this environment can feel challenging but is certainly not impossible.

The discursive context

Some stories will always gain more credence, become more widely circulated and dominant than others, and those of us referred to as professionals hold particular privileges and power. Thus, within hospitals, it is typically the voices and stories of professionals that tend to be heard first, given the largest space, and distributed to the most people. This position allows staff to authenticate some ways of understanding and being, and at times do so at the expense of others; it is a "special authority" that has the potential to impact greatly on a person's life, and not always in ways considered helpful. Thus therapists need to remain mindful of the words they use and the ways in which they choose to use them.

In addition to the storytelling power of professionals, hospital services are in high demand, and accordingly there is an intense pressure to free up beds by moving people through the system. Staff are asked to meet on a daily basis to discuss bed occupancy, and who may be ready for discharge. Arguably, as a consequence, discourses that relate to capitalism, business, and in particular notions of efficiency are now prominent in the way services are organised and run. The medical model appears to lend itself well to this discursive environment by underlying a system geared towards rapid "diagnosis" and "treatment" of a problem, thus enabling prompt return to the community. It may be the case that such ideas run counter to personhood (Strong, 2012), and at times may be at odds to the actual person's hopes and values that are present even in ill health.

Dawn had been referred in relation to making slow progress with her rehabilitation after a life-saving operation. On meeting, it was not long before Dawn said, "I know I should be grateful that I'm alive, but I don't feel like me any more. All I keep thinking about is that I want to do my hair and make-up, but I can't ...". Dawn explained how her appearance was very important to her. She had always enjoyed styling her hair, and had fond memories even from childhood of spending special times with her mother having "pamper nights": doing each other's nails and changing hairstyles. She was also very proud of her home, and had taken a lot of time decorating and furnishing it. Suddenly being in hospital, she found that after her operation her arm movements were considerably limited, and she was unable to take care of her appearance as she once had. Dawn described a sense of dislocation from the many things that she gave value to, and about which she had developed considerable knowledge over time.

How do these ideas try to position therapists?
And what are some of the effects of this?

In settings where medical and business discourses are privileged, therapists may find themselves encouraged to work in ways in keeping with this. For example, they may be invited to assume the role of "expert" to enter a situation and "sort it out"—as well as do so quickly. This is a position that centres the therapist and their knowledge, and in doing so may lessen the knowledge and skills of the person in question. These ideas can also shift how responsibility—for the care of a person—is viewed and held, with decisions around safety and treatment tending to move in the direction of the team. They may encourage more of a "doing to" approach, which can sometimes reduce the perceived importance of gaining informed consent, or even what information is shared.

This is often as a consequence of working towards the agenda of the system as opposed to that of the person. This may help explain why, for many people, they disclose having been unaware of the referral and why decisions about who should be seen tend mostly to be made by staff.

Furthermore, this context supports the frequent switches that can occur in relation to proposed hopes for involvement. For example, initially a therapist might be asked to meet with someone for support, but then the expectation changes, and they are asked to assume more of an assessor role. Thus, to summarise, these ideas can be powerful in shaping expectations about how a therapist should be working, both on the part of the therapist themselves as well as by others, including colleagues and the people with whom they meet.

> Sarah recalled an occasion when she looked at her notes (which were very brief) compared to those written by another team and became very worried that she was not doing what she should be doing. And that her notes implied (to her and perhaps others) that her way of working was not as effective or accomplished as a result of this.

One final but important point

My reflections on discourses prevalent within hospital settings are not intended as an attack or attempt to disqualify certain knowledges. These ideas have contributed to much advancement in the field of medicine and have led to significant improvements in the care, management, and treatment of people living with health problems. Nor do I wish to detract from the high level of support and concern expressed by hard-working members of staff. I simply hope that by making these ideas visible, a therapist is able to consider to what degree they "fit" for them. And whether they would like to assume a slightly different position. Perhaps have a different conversation, or to work in ways that may differ from what is expected.

A different conversation

Thus, if discourse can sometimes serve to narrow, not only the number but the richness of stories available to people in hospital, then I believe an important part of this work is to create space where multiple stories (even if conflicting) can be made visible as well as co-exist. The conversations had with Trudi and her staff team offer an example of what I mean by this:

Trudi, aged forty-four, was referred to psychology after the team reported increasing concern and frustration with her "lack of progress" with walking. Trudi noted that she did want to get back on her feet, but that she felt unsteady when she did so, dizzy and as if her legs would potentially buckle at any point. The team felt that Trudi had already shown that she could walk during her stay on a previous ward, and her recent deterioration was down to "psychological factors": they therefore considered them medically unexplained. Trudi did have a history of accessing psychology services. "Anxiety", "depression", and "eating problems" had been recorded in her notes, and referred to in order to explain what was going on for her currently.

The story as it had been told so far was of a lady who has had multiple difficulties with her mental health, which the team now believed to be responsible for her reported problems with walking. Some of the effects of this story were that it had created a degree of frustration on the part of the team. There was a reluctance to complete any further tests and investigations (as everything so far had come back as negative) and a more general view that if she wanted to improve and get home, then she just needed to try harder. Trudi, by comparison, also reported feeling frustrated, she felt strongly that something had changed with her legs, that they were weaker than before, and that the team did not appear to be hearing this, or believing her. She noted that her biggest worry was not understanding what was going on, she felt frightened by these changes and hoped that, if she understood them a little better, that she might find them easier to cope with.

By sitting and talking with Trudi and thinking explicitly about "multiple stories", it became apparent that she had had a number of serious road traffic accidents in the past ten years, each of which had left her with several physical health problems, including nerve damage, intermittent periods of pain, and swelling in her hip and legs, as well as headaches. Each time she had been hit, she had been so on a particular side of her body, and a recent head scan had picked up an aneurysm that had been present for many years. Prior to her admission, Trudi was receiving physiotherapy for her walking, and they had commented that, rather than getting stronger, her legs appeared to be getting weaker. They expressed a wish to contact her GP so that Trudi could be referred onwards, and this issue looked at in more detail.

The team had completed a number of tests and investigations, but this did not include a review by neurology. The story, therefore, that these difficulties were medically unexplained/psychological had meant that the search for any other potential explanations had ground to a halt. The team reported being unaware of the accidents, and the previous contact with community physiotherapy. Raising this made another story possible: that actually there may be something medical going on for this lady that had not yet been picked up on. It still remained possible that there wasn't, but it felt important that these symptoms were considered seriously and fully investigated before being viewed as medically unexplained. This is one example of another story made visible through talking with Trudi and, with her permission, relaying this to the team.

Another was that through conversation, I came to know Trudi as a person who had been active before the accidents; she spoke of her love of going out and the enjoyment she gained from swimming, biking, and walking. She very much wanted to get back on her feet, to feel stronger, and to find ways to become more active again. Moreover, despite these difficult events, Trudi noted that she felt more "up" than "down" and had found a number of ways to bolster how she was feeling, and keep herself going and hopeful. Relaying this information back to the team (again with permission) presented a further story of Trudi, one of a person who was active, motivated, and very much wanting to improve. Again, this seemed to differ from the first story told, the one that depicted Trudi as a person who would prefer to stay in bed and whose "mental health" was so marked and problematic that it was likely the only reason that could explain what was going on for her.

For the remainder of this chapter, therefore, I intend to consider the following:

- What practically might a therapist be able to do, or think about, in order to side step discourses that endeavour to centre particular understandings, or ways of working?
- What ways are there for space to be created within this setting that allows for multiple stories to be heard and made visible? And how can opportunities for new or alternative understandings, thoughts, responses, and actions be supported?
- How do therapists ensure that the person with whom they are working is always "centred" within their thinking and within

conversations had with the team, and how can preferred ideas and ways of working be kept close?

Moving towards de-centred yet influential practice

Critical to all three of the hopes described is the *de-centred* but *influential* position that narrative therapists aim to adopt wherever possible (White, 2005a). By now, the reader is likely very familiar with this term, but for a re-cap please return to the Introduction.

How can therapists begin to think de-centred before we even meet with a person?

The importance of choice

Medical and business discourse, as discussed, can encourage positions of "expertise" and in turn promote a "doing to" approach. For most therapists, it will feel important to ensure that they work in ways that offer choice wherever they can. Central to choice is for people to have the information they need to make an informed decision; the first decision being whether or not a person would like to meet with you. Lorraine Hedtke's work has taken her to meet with people who are dying, alongside their families. Reflecting on this experience, she noted that people are often "poked and prodded" within medical settings and that, because of this, "she did not want to add to any more possible intrusions by insisting that [a person] speak about things that [they] were not ready to [or] did not want to" (Hedkte, 2000, p. 2).

Within health contexts, it is not uncommon to hear statements like "I feel that Jim could do with bereavement counselling", "Sonia really needs to open up", or "I think this is a delayed grief/trauma reaction". When in hospital and surrounded by others, a person may quickly find that their actions come under intense scrutiny, with family, friends, and staff all offering opinions about what a person should be doing, or what they feel is needed. It is acknowledged that such scrutiny may support the identification of distress and ensure that a person is signposted to relevant services. However, Hedtke's statement serves as a reminder that talking with a therapist has to feel like something that a person wants to do, and workers must, therefore, remain vigilant that a person is not feeling pressured or coerced to do so in any way.

How can therapists begin to support informed decision-making?

Leaflets about the service can be developed and made widely available. This, together with encouraging staff to offer therapeutic services as an informed choice, as opposed to using phrases such as "Why don't you come and talk with the nice lady from our team?" Using standard referral forms can also prompt staff to think about consent by including a section that asks if the referral has been discussed with the person. The form could include information about the therapist's role, as well as ways in which it could be described in order to facilitate understanding. Rob Whittaker (author of this book's documents chapter) suggests including space where the person can record their thoughts, should they wish to. Inviting a person to comment on their own referral may encourage staff to pay particular attention to the language used, as well as the hopes stipulated. It is also important that either within the written information or conversations had that time is spent explicitly thinking about confidentiality. Having a clear agreement about what information can be shared (if any) and the boundaries of confidentiality, as well as the best ways to share it, should be negotiated with a person on a conversation-by-conversation basis.

The importance of timing

> At certain points, you don't want to hear anything bad, as you feel bad enough.

> Quote from Gary

During a hospital stay, people can be faced with considerable changes to their health, feeling very unwell, or trying to adjust to extraordinary circumstances. Kick-starting the process of "talking therapy" may not always be helpful at this point, or even appropriate. Yet despite this, many referrals are made on the basis of concerns about a person's welfare. There can also be very real consequences from time spent in hospital and a person's perceived level of "engagement" with the team. For example, reduced participation in rehabilitation may affect what a person is able to do on discharge, which may determine the level of aftercare needed, and impact on quality of life. It may also influence decisions about discharge destination, including whether a period of additional rehabilitation is considered beneficial. With this in mind, can therapists always step away from getting involved if it does not feel the right time? Or if a person has made it explicit that they do not wish to talk about their experiences? It might be, in a bid to negotiate this complicated position, that therapist and person (or therapist and staff) agree to focus only on those areas that appear to be getting in the way of a person progressing in a direction they prefer.

> The staff were feeling frustrated with Margaret, who seemed to constantly be calling out for assistance and ringing her bell. They suspected that Margaret simply wanted their "attention", and they linked this to information from social care who stated that Margaret had suffered severe neglect whilst living with relatives. Margaret was clear, though, that she did not want to speak to anyone about her experiences. The therapist negotiated with Margaret and the staff, to think in the "here and now" about how they could work together to give Margaret the contact she sought, but also not constantly have their time taken away from other patients and their needs. The therapist facilitated staff and Margaret in developing a timetable of when they would meet; this resulted in Margaret knowing that she could have conversations with staff at regular and predictable times.

Becoming clearer about the concern: what it is, and for whom it is a concern

Unfortunately, there are no easy answers to the complex and, at times, ethically challenging dilemmas of whether to get involved; when?; and in what way? Decisions are complicated further if a person has not given their consent, or is not considered to have capacity to make that decision at that time. Moreover, therapists are obliged to wear different "professional hats" and perform different roles, as reflected on by Fredman, Johnson, and Petronic (2010). They can, therefore, be asked to meet with people not just on the basis of *therapy* but for *assessment* also. I consider the role of "assessor" to be very different to the role of "therapist" or even "supporter/advocate". Consequently, there is a need to delineate, wherever possible and at the earliest opportunity, what exactly is being asked of a therapist and why.

Thus an important first step is to spend time clarifying the hopes of all involved: what is the person aiming for? And are these goals different or similar to other members of the multi-disciplinary team? This process, referred to as "mapping the system" (Fredman & Rapaport,

2010), can support a therapist in thinking about how best to respond. It encourages all parties to remain mindful of the system within which referrals are made, and the request for involvement. It also serves as a guide as to what might be possible, or what might be important to work on or not to consider. Further, it begins to create a space where the person can be centred.

Questions that may support this process include:

Who first identified this issue as a concern? If the person themselves, how did they raise this/talk about this?; if a member of the team, what did you notice, or what encouraged you to think about this, and is this a concern that you feel the person shares also?

What has already been discussed or thought about with the person about this issue?

What led you to take the action that you did to refer? And what did you consider when deciding?

What hopes do you (the referrer) have for my meeting with this person? Do you feel these hopes might be similar or differ from the person themselves? What hopes (as well as worries) do you feel they might have for meeting with me?

If this conversation were to be useful, what would you hope might be different as a result, what new knowledge or understanding might you hope for?

What have you tried before, what has the person found helpful or not so?

What might be important for me to think about before (as well as when) I meet with them?

What if this person does not wish to meet with me, how would you feel about this?

What has it been like thinking about this, what effects (if any) has having these conversations had on the way you might talk with the person and/or on your thinking?

Holding a person in mind

"Holding a person in mind" is a term I first came across within Glenda Fredman's (2014) work, and I now consider it central in supporting de-centred ways of working. It encourages a therapist to always shift their focus towards the person, what is important to them, as well as considering why they are doing what they are doing. Thinking about

Referral information

'Please can you see (name) on (ward), he can be emotionally labile at times, reports feeling low in mood due to his diagnosis, appears to lack insight into the impact of functional limitations on future care needs'. With such brief information it felt important to try to map and explore the referral a little more.

Referrer (OT from the ward)

Fears: that mood is impacting on rehab/that reduced participation will impact on what Tom can do in future and may affect when and how he leaves hospital.

Hopes: for psychology to offer support around diagnosis, to support him to "adjust" to his condition and changed circumstances, to support him to understand the importance of knowing what "realistically" he can do/what life might be like in the future.

To hopefully bolster mood which may enable him to participate more fully in rehab.

Condition Specific Consultant

Beliefs: he will survive, I have met with people who have been living with the same condition and come through it, although I don't know to what extent he will improve.

Fears: he has to take his medication to be able to improve.

Thoughts after mapping

To come and see Tom regularly, for short periods at a time (as that was all he could tolerate), to just be there (unless he told me otherwise), to be a person to listen and think about this experience with him, to be an advocate where appropriate, and try to understand why certain things may feel so difficult. To continue to keep checking with him where I could, that he felt okay talking with me.

Partner of Tom

Hopes: this is such a marked change for him and for us, I know he will get better but need him to believe that also, to feel hopeful and to keep going, to keep trying.

Fears: I am here every day but also have to work, I worry about him being alone. I hope that someone else coming to talk with him will help boost him.

Ward Consultant

Fears: will he survive, do we need to move him onto the palliative care pathway, has he given up, does he feel able to keep going, he is not taking his medication as he should.

Hopes: for psychology to offer support following his change in health, to improve his mood and support his ability to take medication which will help him physically.

Factors I needed to consider/think about

The extent of Tom's change in health which had affected what he could do physically including walking, talking and swallowing. It had affected communication and I had to work harder to talk with Tom.

Fears: I did not want Tom to feel that I was someone who would just turn up and see him when he may not have wanted to see me. However I did not want to not come and see Tom because I needed to listen more carefully/think more creatively about how best to talk with him and hear his thoughts.

I also did not want to become another person to tell him to do things in a particular way, or to be a person that encourages him to "face up to this new reality" when he may not want to think about these types of issues, he may want to hold on to hope that his situation may improve (which it may).

What I later found out from conversations with Tom

Tom reported confusion as to how he had ended up here, how his health could have changed so dramatically and in such a short period of time. Feeling completely dependent on others, which was hard—not knowing how to feel. Not wanting to think about the future, just take each day as it came and trying to get through. Needing to hold on to hope and a belief that his situation would improve/feel easier. That he valued social contact; having someone there he could talk with. Following our meetings, Tom and his partner talked a lot about problems with swallowing which was making taking the medications harder, this was fed back and initially a decision made with Tom to put in a PEG. This helped ensure that he received his medication on time and from this point, his health and function began to slowly improve.

Figure 5.1. An example of mapping the system.

how a person might perceive a therapist can develop this concept further, and the ways in which they might support them to feel comfortable and respected. Fredman suggests workers "examine the pragmatic consequences of their own behaviour and take a position that is both ethical and therapeutic" (2014, p. 37). Thus "holding a person in mind" also encourages reflection on any assumptions that risk entering the conversation (Cecchin, Lane, & Ray, 1992); for example:

What experience has the person had of those working within mental health, medical teams, other services?

What might they be feeling worried or fearful of, what hopes might they have?

What do you know about what they value as well as what they don't within conversations with others?

If you were in their position, what would support you to feel respected and heard?

What ideas and thoughts have you had following this referral, what has resonated with you and how has it influenced you, is this something that feels helpful to draw on or important to be mindful of?

What wider ideas or stories out there might be contributing to how a worker, team, or person is understanding or responding to this situation?

Drawing on work by Burnham (2008, 2012) that encourages people to think about social GGRRAAACCEEESSS [an acronym] can be helpful at this point. For example, considering factors such as gender, geography, race, religion, age, ability, appearance, class, culture, ethnicity, education, employment, sexuality, sexual orientation, and spirituality.

Fredman's ideas also tie into "relational ethics" (Redstone, 2013), which offers an alternative to working only in ways considered ethical by particular organisations or law-makers (rule-based ethics). Redstone instead reflected that preferred ethical practice comes from therapists continually reflecting on their own actions, and those most affected by them, on an action-by-action basis.

Thinking "de-centred" when we actually meet with someone

Setting the scene

Thinking about the environment before therapeutic conversations take place can be helpful. In her work with asylum seekers and refugees,

Lin Lee talks about the creation of a space that is "welcoming", "non-judgmental", and where people are "unconditionally accepted and respected" (2013, p. 3). Whilst most therapists would always endeavour to offer this, there appears to be an added challenge of trying to do so on an acute ward. In spite of this, and similar to Anderson's and Gehart's work on collaborative therapy (2007), I believe that small acts matter and can make a big difference.

> James, aged twenty-two, reflected that he did not like the food served in hospital and, consequently, had not been eating as much as the team had hoped. Yet he recalled one occasion when a nurse commented on him not liking the food and asked if he would like some spaghetti hoops. He still remembers this now, and how much of an impact this seemingly small act of kindness meant to him.

I have tried to incorporate ideas of the "seemingly small" by trying wherever possible to offer choice about where a person would like to meet, for example to stay by their bedside, go to a private room, or off the ward; asking whether the person would like a drink; as well as checking that they have everything they need before starting. Negotiating with people a preferred appointment time is another part of encouraging choice. The hospital invites healthcare staff to just turn up, and while it is important to be able to work flexibly, arriving without a pre-arranged appointment may also add to the feeling of being "done to".

Slowing down, talking about talking

Medical and business discourse tends to encourage speed as people are moved through hospital. Slowing down the process, or "loitering with intent" (Winslade & Hedtke, 2008), is one way by which this position might be slightly side-stepped. Although difficult, and especially so when a person is soon to be discharged, loitering can help create contexts where rich descriptions of preferred life and identity (as well as the problem) can be heard and developed. It also encourages therapists to think about the way conversations are set up, as well as serves as a reminder of the importance of spending time on a topic.

Young, in her work on using narrative ideas within a walk-in clinic, talked about her experience of "slowing down to speed up" (Young, 2006, p. 3); and that even with a reduced amount of time, "narrative practice can lend itself to brief but deep conversations" (Young, 2006, p. 1). Young clarified that "deep" does not refer to an "in-depth assessment, information gathering or searching for truths", but rather "conversations that are deeply meaningful, and therefore create and sustain new ideas, conclusions, visions and hopes" (Young, 2006, p. 2). Thus, in a bid to slow down, create space, as well as remain de-centred, I now consider talking with a person about talking, another important pre-step to therapeutic work (Fredman, 1997; Stott & Martin, 2010). Examples of questions that could be used include:

> Have you talked with someone like me before?
>
> If yes, how did you find it, what did you like, what didn't you like?
>
> If a person has not met with a therapist before, what kinds of talking have you had experience of, for example, with your family, friends, colleagues; which have you found most/least helpful?
>
> What are your thoughts about talking with me? Is this something that you are interested in?
>
> What advice can you give me about "good talking", and how can you let me know if I am doing something different to this, or if our conversation is not feeling helpful for you?
>
> Where did your ideas about good talking come from? Who influenced these?

It can also be helpful to ask a person about listening:

> This question may sound a little strange, but what do you look out for/how can you tell when you are being listened to?
>
> Is being listened to something that you are familiar with?
>
> Who (closest to you) is good at listening, what is it that they do that tells you this?
>
> How can you let me know if you feel that I am not listening carefully enough?

Side-stepping the "agenda"

During therapeutic training, a considerable amount of time is dedicated to the concept of "assessment" and those areas believed important to cover within a first meeting. However, Hedkte's (2000) article serves as a good reminder to try to resist the pull to ask questions on a "psychologist's agenda" and instead take the lead from the person. Thus, by contrast, a therapist could start the conversation by sharing what has been stated in the referral form/discussion. This provides an opportunity to check what fits for a person and what does not, as well as to clarify how much of the information is familiar and what they might consider their main concerns. The following conversational opener was developed from conversations had with Amanda Redstone during training:

Hi Dan,

My name is Louise, I am a psychologist, and I work with people who are in hospital. Were you aware that I had been asked to come and meet with you? Have you ever met with someone like me before?

It is important for me that you feel clear about why I am here so that you can think about whether or not you would like to talk with me some more. The therapists on the ward who have been working with you asked if I could come and see you. They told me that you have recently had to have your leg amputated and that this had come as quite a shock to you, as you had not come into hospital for this reason. They had noticed that you seem to be spending more time in bed, asleep, and not been wanting to join them in rehab as much as before. They were unsure about how you were feeling about everything, whether you have been feeling quite low or worried, and whether this has been affecting you.

Did you know that they had these concerns? Does their story fit or match with your experiences/feelings of being in hospital? What parts fit/what parts do not, or might they have misunderstood or not seen something? Would you like to talk and think with me more about this, or is there something else that feels more pressing for you? Please do not worry, if you are feeling unsure about talking with me, there is absolutely no pressure for you to do so, just take some time and let me or one of the therapists know if you would like to.

Within hospital, therapists will also be asked to meet with people who have experienced changes to their memory or concentration. In such instances, it remains just as important to share with a person the concerns raised by the team, and to check out whether these are worries they share also. The therapist can then discern whether the person is interested in thinking more about this, and if not, their role might be to simply signpost a person to where they can gain support in future. If a person is not thought able to make an informed decision, a therapist may still spend time exploring what a person considers important. This being as there may still be a role to advocate for a person and to ensure, where a decision is made on their behalf, that as much of what they describe as of value to them is encompassed.

Yet the role of "assessor" remains a complicated one, and therapists have to remain mindful of what is required of them as well as the legal and ethical contexts surrounding any assessments undertaken. Exploring what is important to a person will almost always be a useful process, but restrictions placed upon therapists within this role may mean that it is not always possible to work in ways preferred. Furthermore, where concerns pertaining to risk are disclosed, therapists are obliged to act as prescribed by their professional training and relevant local policies and guidance.

Always be thinking about endings

While I endeavour to resist the pressure to work in hurried ways, it is difficult to escape the fact that there remains a real time pressure on the work that therapists do here. They often have to see people quickly and may end up meeting only once or twice before they leave hospital. Lin Lee's ideas of how to respond to premature or abrupt endings were born out of conversations with asylum seekers and refugees who had entered Australia's "detention network" (Lin Lee, 2013, p. 2). She began to wonder if it would be important to treat each session as if it might be the last and to have an explicit conversation about this at the first point of meeting someone. In doing so, Lin Lee felt that goodbyes were always attended to, leading her to coin the phrase "making now precious" (Lin Lee, 2013, p. 8). Rather than closing down conversations, as might be anticipated or even feared, Lin Lee reflected on her "continual [...] surprise" at how such discussions "about endings at the beginning" would "rouse clarity and purposefulness": noting that she would "witness people accepting the invitation with a focused resolve and become precise in articulating what they hoped to speak about, what is most important for them in the moment" (Lin Lee, 2013, p. 8).

One question developed by Lin Lee that can be helpful to hold in mind is: "Do we feel clear about what happens next in the event of meeting again and also if we don't meet again?" (Lin Lee, 2013, p. 4).

Narrative-informed interventions that may be useful within this setting

By this point, you will have likely explored with a person what they consider a concern, if anything, as well as identified whether or not this is a worry shared by others/the team. You might have allowed time to think about how best to talk, and what might help a person feel at ease, comfortable, and respected, so what do you do next? There are multiple possibilities, all of which will depend on what a person might find useful to think about and the direction they would prefer the conversation to take. Within this book, a number of key ideas of narrative practices and maps have been covered, any of which could be thought about here. However, within this setting, I tend to focus on two broad areas of enquiry.

Finding out more about a person and what matters to them most

In Chapters One and Two, it was emphasised that an important part of problem exploration and re-authorising conversations is to get to know a person and the many contexts of their life. Within in-patient settings, this process can help reconnect a person with stories with which they may have lost touch. It may also uncover practices, responses, or experiences that may work to undermine or reduce the dominant story in some way (Lin Lee, 2013). Moreover, sharing aspects of this information with a person's team (if permission is given) can help broaden their view, in that it is humanising and encourages staff to view a person as a person and not simply as a patient.

Simon, a gentleman in his late forties, had been admitted to hospital following a sudden (and unexpected) episode of acute pancreatitis. His pancreas had become inflamed, affecting blood flow, damaging tissue, and increasing his risk of infection and organ failure.

Simon had been in hospital for four months before I met with him. The referral made stated: "Increased anxiety following a fall which is affecting participation in walking and rehab, previously independent with all ADL's (activities of daily living), works full-time and has a young family." Alongside the fall, Simon had also experienced a transient ischaemic attack (small stroke), although most of his symptoms, including slurred speech, had resolved within a week. Simon had not experienced any problems with his health prior to this admission.

First meeting

In our first meeting, Simon described "losing confidence" in walking, and particularly so after his fall. Simon had fallen backwards, hitting his head and bruising his back. He reflected on the length of time he had spent in bed, and how this had affected his strength. Tasks such as sitting or trying to stand now felt effortful for him.

Simon talked about his family; he had two boys and was married to Charlotte, whom he described as a great source of support. He felt worried about his family and, especially, how they were managing financially given that he had been off work for a number of months. His youngest son was finding it difficult to visit his dad, after seeing him so unwell.

Simon talked about worry, and the fear of relapsing. He reflected that each time he began to feel a little better, his pancreatitis would flare up, leaving him "back at square one". Simon spoke about his desire to get home. "Worry" appeared to be getting in the way of this, and Simon was therefore happy to continue meeting to try to find ways to reduce Worry.

Supervision conversation

I had met with Simon on five occasions before I brought him to narrative supervision. I did so, as there appeared to be an unfortunate story developing about him on the ward. The team, including both nursing and therapy staff, had begun to refer to Simon as someone who was "not trying" and "making excuses" to get out of activities they considered good for his rehab. They reflected on occasions when he had cancelled sessions, as he had felt too fatigued or nauseous. They felt he was becoming "hospitalised" and considered him "tiring" to work with. Several staff spoke of "losing their patience". I was unsure to what extent Simon was aware of these ideas, but in our sessions, he too had begun to refer to himself as "weak", "failing", and "letting everyone down". This suggested that he had also started to develop a number of negative (and seemingly thin) conclusions about his sense of himself; thoughts that had not been present prior to hospital admission.

Over time, these stories began to grow in influence, and were now having effects on some staff, for example by discouraging them from popping into his room, answering his buzzer as quickly, or offering as much comfort if he became tearful. For others, the stories seemed to persuade them to step into a parent or teacher role, having long conversations with Simon where they would tell him what he needed to do and why. Worry appeared to have taken more of a hold at this time. Simon continued to spend long periods in bed, and found it difficult to complete many of the tasks and activities asked of him by the team.

Conversations following supervision

The importance of gaining a richer description of Simon's life before admission was emphasised. Time was therefore spent talking with Simon about his job (he worked as a senior figure at a company). We thought about what he did, and how he managed to perform the tasks required of him, what he found helpful when he supervised others, what he valued in his relationships at work, as well as what he felt others valued in the way he supported and managed them.

We also thought about his role as a father and husband and what both Simon and his family enjoyed doing. This included talking about his love of a particular sport of which Simon was a coach. His youngest son enjoyed playing the sport while his oldest was involved in another activity. The family enjoyed going to tournaments on a Sunday, and Simon described his part in ensuring that the family were able to get there on time, at the right place, and arrive well fed and watered.

The relationship Simon had with Charlotte was also explored. Charlotte was present and the couple spoke about what they appreciated about each other, as well as ways they had approached problems that had arisen in the past. Both reflecting that this was not something they had really thought about but usually "just did". There was a noticeable effect of these conversations within the room, with both Simon and Charlotte more animated and appearing to enjoy recalling various stories about life at home. There was also considerably more laughter compared to previous meetings.

The example of Simon highlights the power of creating space for multiple stories of life and identity, outside of hospital, to be heard. By doing so, a safer platform can be developed (White, 2005b), where a person feels more connected to past and current knowledge and skills, as well as to stories of themselves that they prefer. This process can bolster a person and encourage them to think about the concern in question, but in a way that does not simply reaffirm negative identity conclusions (White, 2005b, 2007). This type of work can be useful when time is limited, and reduces the risk of a person being left "unsafe". For example, if a person was to suddenly be discharged home and unable to access the therapist or another service in a timely fashion. Conversations predominately focusing on values, knowledge, and skills may also be helpful if a person does not wish to discuss the concern. They may lead to new understandings or realisations about the problem, without an explicit conversation ever having to take place.

In relation to Simon, these conversations provided a foundation from which he began to reflect on initiatives previously used in difficult situations, and to think about how they could be used in the present. They also made it easier for myself, Charlotte, and Simon to notice when a unique outcome had occurred; one being when Simon managed to reduce Worry, Fear, and Tiredness to the extent that he walked a short distance. We all became curious as to how he had done this and spent time unpacking the skills involved. Simon named the step taken as "Focusing", and by more richly describing this skill and the initiatives contained within it, he began to notice when it appeared to be around, as well as draw on it more.

Becoming reacquainted with a previous view of himself as a person who was competent, organised, and skilled, a view Charlotte, his children, and work colleagues still held about him, was powerful. This view encouraged Simon to challenge some of the more negative conclusions he had been reaching. Moreover, sharing some aspects of these conversations also encouraged a repositioning between Simon and his team. For example, their approach began to shift—it became more compassionate—with many members of staff stepping back from offering suggestions/advice, and instead taking their lead from Simon and what he felt would help. Slowly, and with the support of his family and staff, Simon began to find his feet. He felt more in touch with feelings of confidence and began regularly transferring between his bed and chair, walking more and even practising the stairs. When another flare-up occurred, he described not feeling as worried, stating that instead of worrying, he had been trying to "take each day as it comes" and "think only about the things he is able to change". He found these ideas helpful.

Finding out more about what a person knows about the problem, how they have responded, and the ideas they have in relation to coping with it or its effects

The idea of consulting those who came to therapy offered a very different orientation. It invited me as a therapist to adopt a position of enquiry, to ask questions, to explore the ideas that people have about their own lives ... exploring what is important to those who have come to consult us and the knowledges and skills that they have developed over the course of their lives and experiences (Russell—Dulwich Centre Publications, 2004, p. 30).

Although entire conversations can be had without talking about the problem, it is important to allow space for this, if this is something that a person would like. In such instances, I tend to draw on Statement of Position Map One (as discussed in Chapter One) as a starting point, but I would also enquire as to how a person may have responded and coped with challenges prior to hospital. Thinking with a person about any subtle changes they may have noticed in relation to the problem over the past few days or weeks; for example, its level of influence, intensity, any situations that appear to quieten or exacerbate it, can also be helpful. At this point, it can be tempting for a therapist to provide a person with ideas or information that they feel may help them cope better, for example, psycho-education around anxiety or tips to help regulate their breathing. While these can be helpful, I would always encourage the reader to wait or to be invited before offering suggestions. Moreover, if a therapist does receive permission, I believe that there are ways to do so that help ensure multiple options are offered (as in the next section on advice-giving).

Joshua, aged twenty-three, was admitted to hospital with what initially appeared to be epileptic seizures. However, following further investigation, no organic cause could be found, and Joshua was diagnosed with "non-epileptic attack disorder" by psychiatry.

The "Episodes", as Joshua referred to them, had begun to develop over a number of months, both before and after he experienced two knocks to his head. Initially, he noticed that his body could behave oddly at moments, for example, he could drag his leg, lose his speech, freeze (where he could not move), lose his balance, or become especially sensitive to light and noise.

These experiences developed and worsened over time, and at the point when we first met, Joshua was unable to leave his bed without going into an Episode; sometimes these could last up to three hours. During an Episode, Joshua's body would undergo intense shaking, jerking movements, and he could hit out, or hit himself. At its worst, Joshua reported experiencing over forty episodes within a day.

I worked closely with Joshua, exploring the Episodes and how they had affected him, what was involved, times where they could differ (he differentiated between the bad and not so bad ones), as well as his ideas about what may have led to their development. The Episodes were incredibly debilitating, with even seemingly small tasks such as reading, eating, or having a shower being considerably affected by them.

During the time when we were thinking about ways to try to cope, or reduce their influence, many ideas were banded about as well as tried, often to no avail. However, a significant breakthrough came when Joshua told me about how he had noticed that when he could hear the clock in his room, for some reason, the Episode appeared a little shorter.

He wanted to experiment with this and asked his family to get him a wireless metronome, which he could wear in his ear. By hearing the regular ticking, Joshua found that it helped ground him to what was happening in the present, and he began to find himself beginning to exercise a greater degree of control over the Episodes.

It was understandably a slow process, but with this idea in place, he slowly began increasing activities and the tasks he was undertaking in rehab, and feeling more confident and that more was possible.

The metronome was simply one of several ideas developed by Joshua that had the effect of supporting him to (eventually) shrink the influence of Episodes, and bring them under better control. This was an idea that I would never have thought of, and I doubt other therapists would have, either. I believe this example highlights the importance of ensuring a person is given space to think about the problem at hand, and the knowledge they already possess or are coming to.

The role of information-giving in acute settings: how can this be done?

From a narrative perspective, therapists are mostly discouraged from explicitly giving information. The view being that by doing so, the worker becomes repositioned as expert and this gives greater status to their understanding or way of viewing the world. Yet what can/should a therapist do if a person explicitly asks for their view or opinion? Or what the therapist knows about a certain problem or condition? To not offer anything and merely turn their question back on them might potentially be seen as withholding (another form of using power).

Of course, workers need to think carefully about the information they provide and how they share it, but despite this, I believe it is possible to distribute information in ways that fit with narrative practice. This can be achieved by presenting people with multiple explanations, noting that each is an account or possibility and may not necessarily represent the "truth". Whilst this might not be possible, or feel appropriate for condition-specific information, this practice can be used in relation to many other ideas. For example, if a person asks about the process of grieving—perhaps in relation to them feeling that they are not grieving as they should—then different ideas about grieving and the "nature" of it could be offered:

> There are some theories that believe we go through a number of stages when we lose a person, from anger through to acceptance, that these stages apply to most of us, and that most of us will come out the other end. We just need to work through them.
>
> There are some ideas that question this idea and instead suggest that the loss of a person can be associated with many different feelings and can go on for varying periods of time, with there not being any type of normal or typical way a person should be expected to grieve.
>
> There are some ideas that believe problems can be reduced or their influence lessened by talking about a problem/the loss of a person, whereas there are others that believe that a person does not have to talk about this in order to find peace or a way to go on in life.
>
> There are some ideas that consider ongoing distress as a testimony or tribute to how important a person was for them, rather than being seen as something maladaptive.
>
> There are ideas that remind us that we may have experienced the loss of a person for one, two, three years or more, yet that person may have been in our life for many years more. This might encourage us to question whether we need to arrive at a certain point and/or at a certain time.

From this, you could go on to ask a person:

> Which idea or ideas do you feel most drawn to or struck by?
> You might also wish to explore which explanation seems to fit most with their ideas.
> Or, if none of them, has it left you thinking something else?

Presenting information in this way, and encouraging discussion and disagreement, may lead to new understandings, or alternatively help confirm or thicken particular stories or explanations. Moreover, by rendering visible those practices and ideas that guide a therapist's thinking, the power of the "mental health expert" may be ameliorated, while a person's sense of agency on, and expertise over, their own lives increases. These ideas were developed from conversations had with Amanda Redstone during training.

Creating audiences and opportunities for witnessing and the thickening of preferred stories

Once multiple stories have been identified and preferred stories developed, the therapist is now left to contemplate how such stories can be sustained. This section mirrors the last stage of the re-authoring process; it also connects with ideas discussed by Rob Whittaker on the many ways documentation can be used to thicken preferred accounts. Rather than repeat all that has been discussed within these chapters, I will comment on one additional opportunity I see as present within in-patient settings.

Use of medical notes and documentation

This opportunity comes in our responsibility as therapists working within hospitals to write within the medical notes. Unfortunately, doing so can, at times, encourage relatively thin descriptions of people, or the objectification and marginalisation of their experiences. Yet I believe that there are ways in which something different can be done, and I have been particularly struck by Mann's (2002) reflections on this dilemma. Within her paper, she describes a novel response that includes asking a person to join with her in co-writing their notes. Co-writing of notes helps ensure that the information shared is what the person themselves feels comfortable to share, as well as being done in a way they feel happy with. Co-jointly writing a person's medical notes is not only a respectful and ethical way of documenting, but it can also help bolster preferred stories. Recruiting audiences to witness written information, as well as providing opportunities to widely circulate them, may strengthen such stories further. An example of notes written with this in mind include:

Sally really values social contact and communication and has felt upset when she feels things have not been explained to her, or if staff have been unable to say hello to her in the morning. We both recognise that this is a busy ward and that staff are working very hard, but Sally wanted to let you know that she values this. Sally is aware of tensions that appear to be building between her and staff, and feels that more talking and explaining will help smooth this. Also Sally will frequently doze in order to pass the time, on one occasion she has missed a meal as she was asleep when staff came. Sally would like to ask if there is any way that staff could wake her when her food arrives, she would greatly appreciate this.

In conclusion

I began this chapter by reflecting on issues of power and agency, and I wish to conclude by reflecting on them once more. Hospitals are institutions that all communities rely on, they are valued, and rightly so as they are often there for a person at points in their lives that they might consider their darkest. Yet once admitted to such an established and large system of working, a person's power and agency tend to reduce, and they are required to rely on those around them. While one can never fully step outside of this responsibility, I would encourage therapists to remain mindful of this power and to protect against careless or even harmful misuse. This involves working with a person as a person, to find out what matters most to them, to centre their knowledge and skills, and wherever possible, to move in the direction in which they would prefer both themselves and their team to move.

Note

Please note that I have used a number of words interchangeably when speaking about discourse; terms used include ideas and stories.

Acknowledgements

I would like to thank Amanda Redstone for those first conversations in which we began thinking about narrative ideas within in-patient settings, some of the challenges, and the importance of positioning and de-centred practice. I appreciated encouragement and support from Lincoln Simmonds, and Rob Whittaker for his keen eyes and thoughtful comments.

References

Anderson, H., & Gehart, D. (2007). *Collaborative Therapy: Relationships and Conversations that Make a Difference.* New York: Routledge.

Burnham, J. (2012). Developments in social GRRRAAACCEEESSS: visible–invisible and voiced–unvoiced. In: I. B. Krause (Ed.), *Culture and Reflexivity in Systemic Psychotherapy: Mutual Perspectives* (pp. 139–160). London: Karnac.

Burnham, J., Alvis Palma, D., & Whitehouse, L. (2008). Learning as a context for differences and differences as a context for learning. *Journal of Family Therapy, 30*: 529–542.

Cecchin, G., Lane, G., & Ray, W. A. (1992). *Irreverence: A Strategy for Therapists' Survival.* London: Karnac.

Dulwich Centre Publications (2004). Narrative therapy and research. *The International Journal of Narrative Therapy and Community Work, 2*: 29–36.

Fredman, G. (1997). *Death Talk: Conversations with Children and Families.* London: Karnac.

Fredman, G. (2014). Weaving networks of hope with families, practitioners and communities: inspirations from systemic and narrative approaches. *The International Journal of Narrative Therapy and Community Work, 1*: 34–44.

Fredman, G., Johnson, S., & Petronic, G. (2010). Sustaining the ethics of systemic practice in contexts of risk and diagnosis. In: G. Fredman, G. Anderson, & E. Stott (Eds.), *Being with Older People: A Systemic Approach* (pp. 181–210). London: Karnac.

Fredman, G., & Rapaport, P. (2010). How do we begin? Working with older people and their significant systems. In: G. Fredman, G. Anderson, & E. Stott (Eds.), *Being with Older People: A Systemic Approach* (pp. 31–59). London: Karnac.

Hedtke, L. (2000). Dancing with death. *Gecko: A Journal of Deconstruction and Narrative Ideas in Therapeutic Practice, 2*: 3–14.

Lin Lee, P. (2013). Making now precious: working with survivors of torture and asylum seekers. *The International Journal of Narrative Therapy and Community Work, 1*: 1–10.

Mann, S. (2002). Collaborative representation: narrative ideas in practice. *Gecko: A Journal of Deconstruction and Narrative Ideas in Therapeutic Practice, 2*: 39–49.

120   NARRATIVE THERAPY APPROACHES

Redstone, A., & Fox, H. (2013). *Using Narrative in the Process of Supervision: Level 3 Module Notes*. London: The Institute of Narrative Therapy.

Stott, E., & Martin, E. (2010). Creating contexts for talking and listening where older people feel comfortable and respected. In: G. Fredman, G. Anderson, & E. Stott (Eds.), *Being with Older People: A Systemic Approach* (pp. 87–112). London: Karnac.

Strong, T. (2012). Talking about the DSM-V. *The International Journal of Narrative Therapy and Community Work*, 2: 54–63.

White, M. (2005a). Workshop Notes. http://dulwichcentre.com.au/wpcontent/uploads/2014/01/michael-white-workshop-notes.pdf (accessed 21 September).

White, M. (2005b). Children, trauma and subordinate storyline development. *The International Journal of Narrative Therapy and Community Work*, 3 & 4: 10–22.

White, M. (2007). *Maps of Narrative Practice*. New York: W. W. Norton.

Winslade, J., & Hedtke, L. (2008). Michael White: fragments of an event. *The International Journal of Narrative Therapy and Community Work*, 2: 5–11.

Young, K. (2006). *When all the time you have is NOW: Narrative Practice at a Walk-In Therapy Clinic*. http://www.narrativeapproaches.com/?p=1560 (accessed 17 January).

CHAPTER SIX

Narrative practice and indirect ways of working

Lincoln Simmonds

This chapter discusses how we can apply narrative ideas and practices to indirect ways of working. Indirect work in this context is where the therapist intervenes to support other services and professionals engaged with the person seeking help. It aims to consider how the therapist can integrate narrative ideas into current practices, protocols, and service guidelines. It will discuss areas of work that can be seen to be more distant from the person at the centre: ranging from consultation through to record-keeping with all interventions, seeking to re-orientate conversations back to the people we seek to help. Thus, this chapter is an exploration of how therapists "can scaffold professionals", and others engaged in the work, to develop and thicken preferred stories of the people they support.

Indirect work using narrative therapy involves providing a counter or alternative to dominant accounts of people's problems. Frequently, descriptions and explanations given for concerns in Western society tend to be naturalistic and/or structuralist in their description. Naturalistic descriptions are explanations of problems that cast them as "truths" about a person's "nature", "character", or "self"; for example, "he is anxious", "she is depressed", or "he has a borderline personality disorder". Such descriptions do not extend only to problems but can also be used to describe attributes considered positive as well, for example "she is resilient" (White, 2001). Whether perceived as positive, desirable, or problematic, these are descriptions that view a problem or attribute as a fixed characteristic of a person, something that is internalised and inherent within them.

Structuralist descriptions are derived from generalised socially constructed ideas about illness, problems, people, and the way society feels lives should be lived. Thus diagnoses, or prominent theories about the aetiology and depictions of distress, alongside ideas about how individuals in Western society should be able to achieve things, or overcome difficulties by themselves, often fall into these descriptive categories. Structuralist and naturalistic accounts of problems and identity tend to go hand in hand with both suggesting that difficulties, or indeed achievements, are best explained by structures or deficits that reside within people, and that are in some way part of their biological make-up. For a more in-depth explanation of structuralist and naturalistic accounts, please refer back to the discourse and narratives of illness chapter.

Hazards and limitations of developing (or accepting) purely naturalistic/structuralist accounts of a person's life and identity

Having progressed this far into this book, the reader will likely be familiar with the terms naturalistic and structuralist. They will also be aware that this book does not assert that such ways of describing problems is bad or incorrect. Michael White (2001) wrote clearly about how there is nothing inherently wrong with naturalistic accounts, nor inherently right for that matter about narrative accounts, but rather that therapists can potentially miss opportunities to develop more helpful explanations of people's lives if constrained by a naturalistic lens.

Most psychologists, mental health practitioners, counsellors, and psychiatrists would concede the point that all approaches have their limitations in terms of their explanatory power regarding people's difficulties. Therefore, no one approach can adequately explain the myriad of individual presentations or difficulties. Often, though, practitioners tend not to have such in-depth discussions with the people they see. Nor regularly reflect on the limitations of these models, approaches, and theories in terms of social discourse, power, and the potential effects of their use. Therapists may think about why an approach may have proven unsuitable for an individual with reference to inclusion and exclusion criteria; however, such criteria are often derived from the perspective of a particular approach, and/or described in structuralist and naturalistic terms. For example:

- The person needs to be motivated to do exercises at home.
- The person needs to be at least nine years old.
- They person needs to be "psychologically minded".
- This approach is for low to moderate depression.

There are questions, however, that could be asked of our own and other professionals' theoretical perspectives, or questions that they could be encouraged to ask of themselves:

- Who do you think these ideas most benefit?
- What does this approach say about gender relations?
- What does this approach contribute to understanding other cultures?
- What does this approach contribute to ideas about effective ways of working with people?
- What does this approach infer about how our society affects people and their problems?

How do we offer alternatives, alongside, or counter to, these structuralist/naturalistic viewpoints?

The role of the narrative therapist is to offer a range of possibilities and explanations, a multi-storied account of the difficulties people experience. Think of it as a journey across unfamiliar territory, whereby the person seeking help is given a complete map to work with, as opposed to one set of directions to follow through the wilderness! If a structuralist/naturalistic account of a person's experiences feels most useful and helpful to them, by *their* decision and judgement, then it is the "right" account. Yet if the person feels that it is not a good fit for their lived experience, hopes, and values, then therapists should seek to explore and develop alternatives.

Thankfully, narrative therapists do have a number of tools in their kitbags, which can support the discovery of further possibilities for describing people's lives. Much of what is discussed next has already been outlined in previous chapters. Within this chapter, I seek to think specifically about how these ideas can be used when working with people indirectly.

Externalising conversations

Externalising conversations can be helpful in scaffolding preferred story development. They are not necessarily a requirement of narrative work, but can aid the therapist in facilitating the "unpacking" of negative identity conclusions derived from naturalistic accounts. Just as importantly, they serve as a reminder of practices that run counter to discourses that position problems as intrinsically internal to people. Externalising conversations provide space apart from a problematic storyline, and for a person's experience to be retold as being in "relationship" with problems. Thus, rather than being seen as an inherent weakness or deficit within them, the narrative view conceptualises problems as being separate from people.

The reader is also likely aware that therapists often seek to "personify" or characterise a problem or unique outcome. One simple way of doing this is by putting the word "The" in front of any statements made about it, or referring to the problem as "It". Alan Jenkins (2011) highlighted externalising by considering a structuralist/naturalistic view of resilience in Western society, and countering this from a narrative perspective. He reflected [resilience] "… cannot be orchestrated, possessed or regarded as a personal duality", and that it is more helpful to think about "not what resilience is but what it can do" (Jenkins, 2011, pp. 35–37). Thus what actions can be taken to mediate a person's relationship with resilience? How can they step more fully into The Resilience, if they view it as helpful, and how can they re-negotiate their relationship with The Resilience?

You might be able to see that it is the difference between viewing someone as lacking resilience, or seeking to imbue it *within* them, on one hand, while on the other, resilience is viewed as a concept that will have a particular meaning dependent on the person. For example, the concept of resilience can be considered to comprise many skills and knowledges, and perhaps different skills depending on the situation and context. The narrative therapist would seek to clarify what a person would prefer to do more of or less of, which can lead to increased awareness alongside increased opportunities for preferred action. Thus, by co-researching examples of when the person has used The Resilience to (in their view) the betterment of their lives or the lives of others, stories of using The Resilience in ways considered helpful can be developed and thickened.

THERAPIST: So this Resilience, how does it work with Self Care?

EMILY: Well, I don't know, I can have a bad day at school with my friends, right? And then, it's like, instead of not taking my inhalers like before, I now think to myself "I'm not letting them get to me at home". I'm going to look after me, and have fun with my other friends.

THERAPIST: How is that different from before?

EMILY: Well before, I'd get all depressed and that, and think it's not worth doing my inhalers. But now I think ... I just think about my trampoline club and my friends down the road, and just forget about school and all that crap.

THERAPIST: So what would you call this kind of Resilience?

EMILY: I don't know ... doing other stuff, doing other good stuff.

THERAPIST: Mmmm, that seems like a good name for now ... Doing Other Good Stuff.

Unique outcomes

Another point of entry to preferred accounts is in identifying exceptions to the problem, exceptions which wherever possible would be recognised by the person themselves as unique outcomes. Or of professionals identifying times when they themselves have desired, or taken action, to support the person to develop their life in preferred ways. Or times when the therapist has noticed a person take action or respond in ways that appear to step outside of a problematic account.

> Margaret was extremely early for her appointment. Curious about this, the therapist asked if she and her husband had to go somewhere beforehand, as the therapist knew that Margaret's husband normally drove her. Margaret smiled and said that she had taken the bus, which arrived at that time, and that she had not minded waiting. The therapist noted how pleased Margaret seemed, so more questions were asked. "Is this something that you have done recently, or is it quite a new thing? Why is this so important to you? What does it mean that you've been able to travel here by bus today?" Margaret talked about how, since her accident and the injury to her spine, she had relied solely on her husband for getting around. She had felt very pleased with herself today, and wondered if it related to the problems she had been talking about with her Independence and Confidence since the accident.

The absent but implicit

Furthermore, narrative ideas of the "absent but implicit" can also be drawn on. The absent but implicit helps the therapist remember that people can only talk or know about something in relation to something else. The therapist does this by "doubly listening", that is, paying attention to what something is "not", as well as to what it is. For example, an expression of sadness (what it is) also speaks of someone's hopes for happiness (what it is not). An expression of sadness might also suggest that a person has ideas of what happiness is. Walther and Carey (2009) spoke of listening carefully for the "particularities" or "differences" between events within a preferred story, which was referred to as a "difference between similarities". By doing this, they encouraged the narrative therapist to seek out further deconstructions of normally assumed categories, concepts, or descriptions of living.

Often, one act of something can be assumed to be the same as another, if they are given the same label. However, by accepting this, generalised assumptions about the nature of an experience can be made, and further descriptions and differentiation missed out on. For example, how would different people describe their experience of coping with their condition to others? Would they come out with very similar descriptions, or rather would there be a multitude of stories under the heading of "coping"? Therapists must, therefore, stay alert to the same person having many different accounts and types of a "thing" such as caring. Enquiring about the differing categories may also help expand meaning and develop rich description. For example, "would that act be the same type of caring that you told me about last week, or would you see it as different?"

THERAPIST:	So you said that you were really pleased about the picture you drew after arguing with your school friends on Thursday?
EMILY:	Yeah, it was great. Mum loved it!
THERAPIST:	So was it more of what you called Resilience?
EMILY:	Well, yeah I think so. I mean it didn't stop me taking my medicines . . . .
THERAPIST:	What would you call it? Was it like Doing Other Good Stuff Resilience, or was it something different?
EMILY:	I don't know, it was kind of the same, but kind of different …
THERAPIST:	Oh, ermm … . What would you call it, then? Do you have a name for it?
EMILY:	I don't know, maybe taking my mind off things?
THERAPIST:	Taking Your Mind Off Things … mmm … so how does that work with Self Care? Does it mean there is more Self Care around when you are Taking Your Mind Off Things?

Applications of narrative ideas in specific contexts

Consultation

This section examines situations where other professionals/services are seeking to consult with the therapist about a person(s) with whom they are working. Particular discourses tend to dominate within such consultations, for example, expectations of the mental health professional holding the "expert opinion" can often take the foreground. At other times, there can be an expectation that the mental health professional or service needs to work with a person, and perhaps needs convincing to "become involved" through the process of consultation. The hazards are that both positions can lead to conclusions that may be unhelpful to a person, and diminish both their preferred identity narratives, as well as those of the professionals working with them.

It is important to acknowledge that those seeking consultation are often in situations where they feel "stuck" or overwhelmed. Of course, mental health professionals do have knowledge, skills, and experience that can help understand and resolve such difficulties. However, where dominant discourses of "expert opinion" are prevalent, professionals tend to be guided to think that neither they nor the people at the centre of the work have anything to offer other than giving information to the mental health expert, to form an opinion. Such discourses can also suggest that the mental health service needs to be "doing" something, and this can lead to the diminution of the contribution of the professionals involved. It can also result in such professionals contributing to discourses in which they see themselves as playing no further role, or that they have exhausted their skills and resources to no avail. This discourse can also suggest that the person needs "specialist help" in order to resolve, or perhaps even contain, their difficulties as their situation goes beyond what is considered "normal" experience.

> Do you ever encounter these dominant discourses in terms of you being put in a position of expert, or being viewed as withholding a service/solution by other professionals?
>
> Are there times when this has been helpful to the person or medical team?
>
> Are there times when it has been unhelpful to the person or medical team?

At times, a mental health professional may have to work very hard indeed to counter such views, but using narrative ideas and perspectives can be particularly helpful here. The narrative therapist may first seek to deconstruct the idea that the mental health professional is the "sole expert" in the room. This can be difficult, but doing so can help create a context in which others' thoughts and experience are given weight within the conversation, and this is often a helpful starting point. The therapist can do this by making explicit efforts to enable colleagues to remain aware of their knowledges and skills. Emphasis is given to how important these are in developing an understanding of the person and the difficulties described. It is often useful to view colleagues as experts in being able to help those present understand the experiences of the people at the centre. Often, it is important to contextualise, or re-contextualise, the consultation space as a "thinking space" in which it is emphasised that everyone participating can bring ideas, thoughts, and stories to share. Previous experiences of formal meetings may need to be deconstructed here, suggesting that people are welcome to share unformed ideas or images as opposed to just "facts".

Of course, the main challenge to such an invitation is to keep the discussion firmly centred on what the people whom we are seeking to help (or even the team) would find useful, as opposed to giving priority to the reproduction of existing explanations for people's difficulties. This is the central aim of the narrative consultation process. It is commonplace, though, for such conversations to take place without the person who is the subject of the discussion being present. Whether or not we should actually have consultations concerning people in their absence is perhaps a matter for discussion outside of the realms of this chapter, and obviously there are hazards in doing so. The facilitator of the consultation needs, therefore, to be very active in ensuring that the conversations contribute towards preferred story development of the person professionals are trying to help. At times, it may be necessary to steer the conversation away from tendencies to theorise, or hypothesise, about the person and their relationships. The "right" or preferred story will always be the one preferred by the actual person, *not* the professionals around the person, and it is this story that the therapist seeks to thicken within consultation. There are exceptions to this, though, and of course the therapist is accountable to upholding practices that ensure that other people's values, rights, and safety are preserved. Thus stories that run counter to this will not be supported, even if they are seemingly preferred by the person at the centre.

As stated earlier within this chapter, eliciting externalised descriptions can often lead to an increased sense of personal agency, and the therapist bearing witness to richer and thicker descriptions of people's lives (White, 2000, 2004). It is also helpful to seek out exceptions to the dominant problem story, also referred to as unique outcomes. Thus, it is important to ask colleagues seeking help about the person's interests, hobbies, positives relationships, and hopes. Referring to what the person would say about the consultation (particularly in their absence) can help bring the focus back to the person's experience, thus realigning professionals to centre the consultation on the person. Such story development also gives scope to identify or envisage the person's values, hopes, skills, dreams, and knowledges, to further develop into preferred stories of their life. By acknowledging ways in which professionals are already acting that are helpful to the person, the therapist may support development of preferred accounts of professional identities also.

Of course, all of the above discussions need to be carried out in ways that translate into tangible actions/steps that the professionals seeking help can take. This would be the desired outcome of any such consultations. It would also be important that the therapist feeds back the discussion to the person seeking help, if they are not able to be present. Narrative therapeutic letters or documents that use externalised statements, and highlight preferred accounts, can be particularly helpful in this respect. Such documents can be co-written by the professionals seeking help with guidance from the therapist, on the explicit agreement that the person is the "editor" of the document/letter, and that they can amend/change it and seek clarification, if needs be, on receipt. This would need some consideration in terms of how professionals normally document, record, and formalise consultations through written correspondence, and there are a number of suggestions later in this chapter.

Example

A team of care workers in an emergency respite provision for young people in crisis came to a consultation. We externalised "Loneliness" and "Rejection" as affecting a young person with chronic juvenile arthritis in particularly problematic ways: in terms of how they viewed themselves, and the relationships between the young person and staff. Through using the outsider witness scaffold, the professionals were able to make guesses about what the young person gave value to, or hoped for. They gained further insight into that which was being blocked by the Loneliness and Rejection, which seemed to be a sense of Connecting with other young people and Having Fun. They empathised by relating their own experiences of struggling with Rejection and Loneliness, and then were able to identify ways in which they could make changes in their work with the young person in order to develop Having Fun and Connecting in his life. These stories were based on newly perceived unique outcomes of Connection and Fun, which ran counter to the Loneliness and Rejection.

Conducting meetings

Meetings between people we seek to help and professionals can be adapted in order to work towards developing preferred storylines. I have used adapted forums when the "usual" types of meetings have failed, or where the person has disengaged from the process. Assumptions behind this have partly been based on struggling to overturn dominant discourses of how meetings "should" be. Meetings are usually run along prescribed lines, which invariably meet the expectations of the professionals/organisation, as opposed to primarily the needs of the person. Though this more dominant format can be helpful and useful to people; in those instances where it is not, an alternative forum is needed.

While it is important to recognise that some meetings have to be conducted along prescribed lines, particularly in the context of tribunals or safeguarding issues, other parallel meetings can still be conducted to supplement, influence, or address issues perhaps marginalised by some of these more dominant structures. It is possible that many professionals view the "normal" format as centred on the people we are seeking to help. Indeed, various strategies or measures are usually taken to try to prioritise this, for example, the use of advocates, allowing comments from the person, the distribution of minutes and reports prior to the meeting, and so forth. This section, however, aims to outline steps for conducting meetings where this focus is made even more explicit.

First, state to the attendees that you are holding a "different" type of meeting. It is very important to "lay the context" in terms of setting out how such a meeting may differ from the norm. I would initially aim to have the person whom the team are seeking to help set the agenda. Of course, people cannot be expected to necessarily know how to do this. Hence you are advised to view this as a way of facilitating the person in deciding the agenda. I have found the following structure to be helpful.

The person selects whom they would find helpful to attend such a meeting, so in essence they select their "team". Participant professionals are invited and told that it is a "different type of meeting"; they are given information on the format, what is expected of them, and the likely role of the facilitator. The facilitator is given permission to interrupt! Interrupting to re-guide the conversation in a direction that supports preferred narratives is allowed. White (2007) might refer to this as a determination not to "relinquish" the meeting to unhelpful discourses! The person is interviewed in front of the professionals. What is important to the person is highlighted alongside preferred directions for the person's life and unique outcomes.

The professionals are then interviewed to seek out their resonant responses, using the outsider witness scaffold. However, the transport question (category four on the scaffold map) would primarily be focused on how professionals might now act with their increased understanding of the person and their experiences. For example: "Having listened carefully to the conversation I've had with Mark, has it given you any ideas about you might support Mark in being able to Do Things For Himself? What might you do differently here on in?"

The meeting is concluded by a summary that is co-written with the person. This document is then sent out with "actions" for supporting the person's preferred stories, or just as important the preferred stories of other people who may struggle with similar difficulties.

Example of application

I suggested to the various parties involved that an alternative forum might be more helpful to a young person (Alex). Alex had disengaged from various services' usual means of helping, yet there remained considerable concern about his welfare and future.

I thought carefully with Alex about the type of meeting, or discussions, which would be most helpful to him. Together, we identified a number of values and hopes for his life, which he hoped to be supported into developing further. These hopes related to being able to Work on Art, Feel Safe at College, and Have His Say in clinic.

Alex and I felt that the format, where I interviewed him about these hopes and values (based on previous conversations in individual work), would be the most useful one to use. This set-up enabled professionals to be placed in a position of listening, and I could manage how they responded so that it could be as useful as possible. I would also seek to manage what Alex considered unhelpful "advice", "telling off", or "lecturing" from professionals.

As part of the preparation, professionals and adults who were attending were asked for their "permission" to be steered away from topics or conversations that Alex was not interested in. I was given permission to interrupt if necessary, as well as to ask "set" questions based on the outsider witness scaffold. Flip-chart sheets were provided to support responses to Alex's values, again in ways that followed the lines of the outsider witness scaffold (see the chapter on working with children and young people).

In addition to this, Alex and I asked the professionals: "In what ways can you support this hope, or this value, that Alex feels is important in his life?" Alex was particularly surprised to hear that the clinic staff were actively encouraging him to state what he wanted within clinic appointments, and that they were keen to hear from him about anything they could do to make it easier to attend and speak more freely.

Lastly, it was decided that the meeting would be documented with a narrative letter based upon the interview and flip-chart responses; Alex was able to edit this as well as decide with whom to share it. Actions generated from the discussion were decided upon and communicated with those involved; the overarching view being to support Alex to more easily "access" and "step into" emerging preferred storylines.

Record-keeping

In relation to documentation, ask yourself:

> Is there room to negotiate record-keeping standards to meet the requirements of the person as well as my employer/organisation?

This negotiation would be to see if there is potential for the person to be an author (to some extent) of their own notes. The therapist could write notes as they usually do but allow the person to review them, alongside a chance to document their comments. The person could be encouraged to dictate notes for themselves, while making it clear (within the record) that it is the person's document/entry as opposed to the professional's. Alternatively, co-written notes could be developed within sessions, with who has written also distinguished. This clarity of authorship would not only be for obvious medico-legal reasons, but to give the person a clear sense of ownership of their retellings. It may also provide scope to enquire, within the limitations of organisations, how people would like therapists to keep their notes. People can often prefer pictorial forms, whilst some may prefer an audio recording. These ideas also beg the question of how professionals make note-keeping accessible to those with learning disabilities, neuropsychological difficulties, or literacy problems. At the very least, it would be interesting to debate this with the people the therapist sees, and their colleagues within their organisations.

Using electronic and virtual contexts

The therapist can contact professionals by email or letter in order to seek out specific responses that support preferred narratives. Of course, professionals will need to adhere to confidentiality guidance and service protocols in using such mediums. Yet in relation to this practice, it is also important to establish the context, by explaining the usefulness of the exercise to the person seeking help. The worker can use questions co-developed with the person during sessions. Another idea would be to use questions based on categories of enquiry from the re-membering map (White, 1988, 1998):

What do you appreciate about the person?

Can you tell me a brief story that exemplifies what you appreciate about the person?

What have you learned about the person during your work that has pleasantly surprised you?

What do you know about what the person sees as important?

What do you know/or can guess about the person's hopes and dreams?

Can you identify anyone who is particularly supportive of the person's hopes, dreams, or what he/she values?

Example of application

A therapist asked a medical ward team what they appreciated about Jenny. Jenny was a young person with a cardiac condition. Staff talked about how they observed how caring Jenny was. She always asked after the nurses when she came to clinic, and at times had brought them confectionary to share. On one occasion, one member of staff had been particularly touched when Jenny had given her a card, after the staff member's mother had died. It became more apparent that it was important for Jenny to see herself as a person who could connect with and support others, even despite her debilitating condition. Previously thinking that Jenny's only concern should be about her own quality of life, the medical team had never considered that helping others gave Jenny considerable significance to her life. To this end, they began to explore whether Jenny would value a role as a "buddy" to other young people who were struggling to cope with the effects of their conditions.

Peer supervision

I have speculated over whether it is possible to devise a professionals' peer supervision group which acknowledges the diversity of experience, theoretical backgrounds, personalities, and life experiences of participants, without allowing a particular model or practice to dominate above others. How can professionals avoid situations in which people holding positions of greater power and responsibility have their contributions more highly valued than others within a supervision group? And how can professionals avoid some voices or stories from becoming marginalised or unheard? Often, those in question are those belonging to people that may be viewed as having less "expertise" or less formal mental health experience. Once again, outsider witness practices can be incredibly useful and offer a framework by which peer supervision can be constructed and run to directly counter such concerns.

For a number of years, I was fortunate enough to be part of a peer supervision group which was facilitated by Hugh Fox. Hugh has written an engaging paper on using the outsider witness scaffold within peer supervision (Fox, Tench, & Marie, 2002). I have found this experience invaluable in terms of helping me in my work and in "staying true" to the values I would describe as my preferred professional narratives. It was hard to narrow a work application down to one, let alone an example that I could share in this chapter with the permission of the people at the centre of the story. However, looking through my notes of supervision groups I had attended, it was clear that the sessions facilitated me in bringing my experience of the work as close as I could to the experience of the people with whom I was working.

Indeed, it was often when I had become fixated on what I felt "should be happening or I should be doing" that I tended to find myself having become stuck. These "shoulds" tended to be made up of descriptions, explanations, and dominant theoretical perspectives, so in essence, were times when ideas from my psychology training took "centre stage". Unfortunately during such times, rather than help me or offer particular insights, these ideas could occasionally stand in the way of my thinking. It was then that the outsider witness scaffold would support me to steer back to the person's preferred accounts and what they might consider helpful, as opposed to mine and/or dominant ideas of mental health from a Westernised perspective. Thus, within peer supervision groups, I would encourage the facilitator to:

Make space to deconstruct taken-for-granted ideas.
Empower marginalised people and their voices.
Value the diversity of experience and different knowledges.
And place the people we are seeking to help firmly at the centre of the supervision sessions.

I have previously outlined (Simmonds, 2006) guidance for conducting a narrative peer supervision group. It is important to think about the maximum number of people with whom the facilitator will feel comfortable working. It may also be important to think about the membership of the group. For example, if the approach is unfamiliar to many attending, then it might be better to seek a commitment from participants that, over a period of time, they will familiarise themselves with some of the ideas and the outsider witness framework. Within this format, a therapist/worker will bring an issue, dilemma, or material and will then be interviewed about it. Often, the group facilitator would limit such conversations to one or two pieces of work over a ninety-minute period. The rest of the group would discuss their responses to the work through being interviewed by the facilitator using the outsider witness scaffold. The facilitator would then return to the worker to seek their responses to the comments made by the listeners. Then all the therapists would talk together about the process of carrying out supervision in this way. For more information, please see Michael White's workshop notes (www.dulwichcentre.com.au website) which provides further questions to support exploration using the outsider witness framework, and Fox, Tench, and Marie's paper written in 2002.

Outline of the outsider witness scaffold that can be used in peer supervision

First category: Eliciting the expression, i.e., "What caught your interest? What struck you about the conversation you just heard?"

The *second category* is in two parts:

Bringing forth an image, i.e., "Does any particular picture or image about the person and their situation come to mind?"

Inferring what the person discussed gives value to, i.e., "What does it tell you about what is important to this person?"

The *third category* seeks to connect the outsider witness's experience to that of the person at the centre by seeking resonances, i.e., "Does this strike a chord with your own life or work?"

The *fourth category* is that of transport, whereby the facilitator seeks to elicit what effects there have been on the outsider witness, i.e., "Has this conversation taken you anywhere? Having heard this, what do you think you might do, or think about differently?"

In order to facilitate people who may be unfamiliar with this approach, often the facilitator can take the lead in the initial sessions, in interviewing the therapist and supporting other members of the group to provide resonances as per this format. The facilitator may also find it helpful to give people advice and tips to help them adapt their normal supervisory interviewing style to fit more with the outsider witness approach. Suggestions, for example, may include:

Slowing down the pace of the interview.
  Asking fewer questions.
  Paraphrasing and summarising for clarification.
  Thinking aloud, i.e., being transparent in thought processes.
  Asking the interviewee (person bringing the work problem/dilemma) what effects the problem/issue has had on them.

In conclusion

The ideas discussed in this chapter are ways of disrupting the course of conversations that may have become overly focused on the therapist (acting as consultant) as the expert on other people's lives. They are ideas that seek to reconnect professionals with the person who is seeking help. Such contexts can provide space to deconstruct problematic descriptions, and in doing so make room to thicken a person's preferred ways of living and seeing themselves.

This chapter does not suggest that the "solutions" to overcoming, dismissing, or diminishing problem stories reside solely within the person at the centre. Indeed, a narrative stance emphasises ideas of connection in terms of how our lives, experiences, and stories touch one another, and how crucially we can act in ways that are supportive of each other's preferred accounts. The narrative consultation, therefore, would seek to engage team members to work together in practical ways to thicken such preferred narratives. This chapter does not argue (as is an often-levelled criticism of narrative therapy) that consultants/ therapists should not use their power at all. Rather, it puts forward that narrative therapists should remain explicitly aware of the dynamics and relations of power within the consultation, and seek to use their influence in a transparent manner, whereby they adopt a decentred but influential position, as discussed in earlier chapters.

From such a position, the therapist may not only bear witness to rich story development in the lives of the people they seek to help, but also of colleagues that are seeking help. Often, colleagues may report frustration and despair about a problem situation, because it not only affects the person at the centre, but can obstruct and perhaps disconnect them from what they value in their work with people. Within consultations, there are opportunities to reconnect professionals with their preferred ways of working too; ways that often fit with how people seeking help wish to be viewed and related to by professionals.

Acknowledgements

To my family, for reminding me of the importance of thickening preferred aspects of our family's story, thus reminding me that there are other far more important preferred stories to develop other than writing a book.

References

Fox, H., Tench, C., & Marie (2002). Outsider-witness practices and group supervision. *The International Journal of Narrative Therapy and Community Work, 4*: 1–13.

Jenkins, A. (2011). On becoming resilient: overturning common sense—part 1. *The Australian and New Zealand Journal of Family Therapy, 32*: 33–42.

Simmonds, L. (2006). Peer supervision where everyone has a voice. *Narrative Forum, 3*: 1–3.

Walther, S., & Carey, M. (2009). Narrative therapy, difference and possibility: inviting new becomings. *Context, 105*: 3–8.

White, M. (1988). Saying hullo again: the incorporation of the lost relationship in the resolution of grief. *Dulwich Centre Newsletter, Spring*: 7–11.

White, M. (1998). Saying hullo again: the incorporation of the lost relationship in the resolution of grief. In: M. White & D. Denborough (Eds.), *Introducing Narrative Therapy: A Collection of Practice-Based Writings* (pp. 17–29). Adelaide: Dulwich Centre Publications.

White, M. (2000). *Reflections on Narrative Practice: Essays and Interviews.* Adelaide: Dulwich Centre Publications.

White, M. (2001). Narrative practice and the unpacking of identity conclusions. *Gecko, 1*: 28–55.

White, M. (2004). *Narrative Practice and Exotic Lives: Resurrecting Diversity in Everyday Life.* Adelaide: Dulwich Centre Publications.

White, M. (2007). *Maps of Narrative Practice.* New York: W. W. Norton.

CHAPTER SEVEN

Narrative practice and the written word

Rob Whittaker

I went to see a young man on the intensive care unit at the large regional hospital where I was working as a psychologist. Craig had multiple chronic illnesses and had been known to staff at the hospital all of his life. I knew of him by reputation, though had never met him myself. I had been told on more than one occasion that he was "very unwell"—a euphemism on the unit for "dying"—only to see him a week or so later, oxygen cylinder in tow but as chirpy as you like, enjoying a coffee at one of the retail outlets on the ground floor of the hospital. Craig had respiratory problems as well as kidney failure, and lived a precarious existence hinging on the variable effectiveness of his treatments in stopping fluid filling his lungs. His life over recent years had been punctuated by multiple near-death experiences.

The nurse who asked me to go and see him expressed concerns about his periodic "catatonia". She described these episodes as times when he was conscious but completely unresponsive and these were becoming more frequent. The nurse told me that several members of the ICU staff were very concerned about his mental health. She said they had wondered whether Craig, despite his generally cheerful demeanour, was deeply depressed, or even experiencing some kind of psychosis.

I went to see him and, after a bit of chat about the game he was playing on his iPad, we started talking about what it was like being on ICU. He told me it was generally really boring but occasionally really scary. He said that the beds were arranged such that the patients could not see one another but they could hear things. He had heard what he assumed were other patients dying.

I told him about the conversation I had had with the nurse about times when he was awake but unresponsive. He said he knew what I meant. I asked him what he would call this—he said "I go into my shell". I asked him what this was like for him: when he was in his shell. He described it as a peaceful place, with no worries, no pain, no noise even. He said that when he was looking out from his shell, he was aware of what was happening but entirely untroubled by it. I said it sounded like it might be quite an important place to go from time to time, and he agreed.

I asked him if he had noticed anything else about this going into his shell that he thought was important. He thought for a while and said that it was particularly likely to happen on the morning of days when nothing was going to happen—no tests, no trips off the ward, and no visitors until the evening.

I asked him what he thought it was like for others—his parents, for example, or the staff on the ward—when the shell came over him. He hadn't given this any thought before and considered the question for some time. He said he thought it was probably quite worrying and confusing for people. I asked what it was like for him to think this, and he said that he didn't like to think of other people being worried for him. He was particularly concerned about those times when he was in his shell as it really wasn't anything for others to worry about.

I asked him about writing an entry in his notes to help staff not worry about him when he was in his shell. He said he thought this was a great idea, but didn't imagine it would be allowed. I went to the nurses' station and asked for Craig's notes. Craig dictated and I wrote:

Dear staff
I am writing to let you know some important things about times when I go very quiet and don't respond when you talk to me. The first thing I want to say is that when I go into my shell like this I don't want you to worry—I'm ok, it won't last long, I'll come out of it in a

while, there's nothing you can do to get me out, I'll come out when I'm ready. I do notice you there so do keep coming and being with me.

Thank you

Craig

(With the help of Dr. Rob Whittaker, clinical psychologist)

We drew lots of stars around this entry in the notes. I also asked the sister in charge if she could make sure that staff on shift were aware of it and that it be mentioned in the next couple of ward handovers. I didn't see much of Craig over the next year or so. However, when I did see him, he said he still hadn't gone back into his shell since our meeting.

This story exemplifies a number of narrative practices that are of great importance to working with people with physical health problems. As workers with professional titles such as "Dr.", and especially within medical settings, psychologists in particular but therapists in general are invested with considerable power. Therapists are encouraged not to attempt to deny this power (White, 1997) for to do so encourages the risk of using it to oppress others, however unwittingly. My position as a psychologist affords the opportunity to use this power to privilege the voice of the person being seen. It also affords the possibility to document their knowledge, ideas, and expertise (Mann, 2002). These documents can then be circulated among relevant healthcare staff. Such documents are important and influential contexts of the life of the person at that time.

This process is deeply respectful of people: it promotes their sense of personal agency and constructs and circulates stories of their identity as competent, trustworthy people whose knowledge and opinions are important and of value. This construction of the person runs counter to the common cultural practices of patienthood, where the person must be passive, deferential, and obedient, and whose knowledge is not regarded as important beyond that required to make a diagnosis, monitor symptoms, and so on. Frank (2013) refers to the process of "narrative surrender" as people become patients—they relinquish their storytelling rights to the professionals under whose care they fall. Narrative practitioners in a medical context aim to subvert this process.

Narrative practices of documentation

Much has been written about the purposes and practicalities of narrative practices of documentation, and I would direct interested readers to two particularly excellent sources (White & Epston, 1989; Fox, 2003)—both of which provide extensive examples—rather than summarise them here. *Narrative Means to Therapeutic Ends* remains an extraordinary book. A good half of the book is made up of letters from either Michael White or David Epston. One particularly engaging letter is as follows:

> Dear Fred
>
> Are you surprised to be getting this letter? I'm surprised that I'm sending it. It's just that yesterday I was distracted by a person doing push-ups in the park and I tripped over a gutter and stubbed my toe. What has this got to do with you? Well, at our last meeting, I remember that you had a sore foot. My hurting my toe jolted me into thinking of your foot, and this in turn had me wondering how you are doing. That's all.
>
> > See you at the next meeting.
> > M. W.
>
> (White & Epston, 1990, pp. 123–124)

This unassuming, playful letter makes the important point that narrative therapy relationships are highly personal relationships between two human beings—unconstrained by the professional practices of distancing, dividing, and one-upmanship.

This letter is also a good example because it is so brief! Working in the NHS (and likely most other publicly funded agencies), with its dwindling budgets and increasing demands, is characterised by a pervasive sense of never having enough time to do anything properly. Students often state that they do not have time to write great long letters to clients because they barely have time to do what is required of them, let alone this kind of "optional extra" after the session. However, such a point is often premised on the idea that only a long, finely crafted letter will do. How long will Michael White have taken over the above? The document constructed with Craig was part of the session. Objections are often also premised on the notion that clinicians have enough letters to write to referrers, GPs, and other colleagues without these additional tasks. Over the years, services have debated whether patients should be copied into letters about them. In line with Fox (2003), this logic can be flipped for the therapist to write primarily to the person, and ask if they are happy for the letter to be copied to the referrer. However, in some agencies, the bureaucratic strictures are such that this may not be possible.

It is arguable, though, that therapists should write letters that are written specifically for the person as opposed to other professionals. The question then becomes what kinds of letters should therapists write, and to whom? And indeed what other forms of written communication might offer opportunities for the circulation of the preferred stories of people's lives?

This chapter will describe a number of different ways to engage with these ideas in healthcare settings. This chapter will at first continue by considering the ethics of written documents in therapy.

Ethics and the written word

Letters draw their power through their permanence and the authority in our culture of the written word, particularly if written by a professional (Epston, 1994; Parry & Doan, 1994). The profession of clinical psychology, among others, has an inglorious history of using this very power to condemn, to pathologise, to limit, to constrain, to insult, and to blame. There are therefore significant risks inherent in committing words to paper, so narrative therapists must pay particular attention to the politics of the practice of writing.

Putting experience into words, particularly experience of illness, is at once a representational and a constructive act. Rendering our lives into narrative gives order to the complexity of living, and linearity to the chaos of subjective experience. This is a core and vital function of narrative (Frank, 2013), particularly when stories relate to the non-verbal aspects of embodiment. Thus, therapists must be particularly cautious when taking responsibility for transposing dialogue, with its shifting, nebulous, rhizomatic complexity, into necessarily linear, authoritative, and permanent text. To write a summary of any conversation is to stop time, to stop the "ramification" of time (Duval & Béres, 2011), to close down possibilities, to edit out so much potential. To do this with the stories of someone else's life from a position of authority is a hazardous endeavour.

As with so many ethical dilemmas in therapeutic work Michael White's ideas about the position of the therapist helpful can be helpful in negotiating these hazards (see Morgan, 2006). In line with White's ideas, the narrative therapist is encouraged to ensure that letters remain centred on the knowledge of the person, while maintaining ethical responsibility as editors to structure the documents with a particular intentional stance. The person's voice may reproduce dominant, oppressive, normative, deficit-laden narratives at times. The narrative therapist must therefore take care to chart a course between acknowledging the problem story/stories and avoiding lending them further power through reifying them in the written word. Explicitly and transparently stating which editorial choices have been made in narrative therapeutic letter can be helpful:

> Dear Joy,
> We have talked, as you know, about many things in our meetings but I am writing just to summarise a few of them, as we agreed last time. I would be very interested to hear any thoughts you have about this letter, including if you think I've missed anything important or misunderstood anything.
> Much of our conversation so far has been about your family. You have told me about the ways in which your parents have treated you over the years—often very bullying, abusive, perplexingly hostile, unreasonably untrusting, and hurtful ways. It is my sense that cataloguing these ways in more detail would serve to make this a very bleak letter—suffice to say, you have been treated in ways that are in my opinion appalling and utterly unfair.
> I have been particularly interested, Joy, in your responses to this treatment. You could, I suppose, have learned from your experiences that treating people in these kinds of ways is ok, what is so striking about you, Joy, is that you have resolutely refused to emulate your parents' ways of treating people. You have told me that some years ago, you made a vow to yourself: "I don't want to be like them". I asked you how you prefer to treat people. You told me that the following things are important to you …

Even if we can resist the replication of dominant problem stories in our letters, therapists would be strongly advised to work hard to keep a multitude of alternate stories alive, rather than limit the territory to just one. The written word is frozen in time—once a word is written down, there is no room for amending it—all further negotiation is precluded. Therapists cannot conflate this finality of expression with certainty of meaning. However, a letter, just as much as a spoken utterance, is a turn in a conversation (albeit asynchronous). The reader may well engage with and interpret the meaning in a whole range of ways. White and Epston (1989) advise us to adopt the "subjunctive mood"—a tentativeness, our sentences full of "mights" and "maybes"—and this seems particularly important in written communication, especially when we are introducing some of our own ideas, and making links. Jim Wilson, talking about written documents addressed to children says, "things can be said as 'wonderings' that allow time for the child to think about them. There is no need for an immediate reaction" (Wilson, 1998, p. 91). A subjunctive mood keeps the dialogical process alive.

Narrative therapists should be tentative in their approach to letter writing, and do what they can to anticipate the meaning the reader will make of the words. Therapists can attend to how the person is positioned in the letter through the language used: in what ways is the letter constructing the person, their life and relationships? As in therapeutic conversations, therapists seek to strike a balance between using the person's words and offering up alternatives for consideration. Although this is not fully consistent with the decentred position of the narrative therapist, I feel that it is legitimate to include words, ideas, and questions that did not form part of the conversation, but it is important to remain clear about the intentions behind the words used.

These suggestions along with the references cited may suffice for the reader to be able to write summary, "keeping-the-story-alive" letters that can be the mainstay of letter and document writing in narrative practice. Often, conversations with people who are referred with "difficulties adjusting" to illness (newly diagnosed diabetes, for example, or the after-effects of a heart attack, or a downturn in respiratory function in someone with cystic fibrosis) will barely touch on the physical health problem in conversation. The person wants instead to talk about their thoughtless boyfriend, their critical mother, their abusive father, their problems with substance misuse, and so on. This is a salutary reminder of the multi-storied nature of life, and the complexity with which ill-health interweaves with other aspects of life, relationships, and identity. Illness stories can overshadow other stories, and it is important for therapists to keep an ear open to the other stories of life that the person may wish to address. Often, addressing other difficulties in people's lives can have a powerful influence on their relationship to illness, with a positive impact on their "adjustment" or their "adherence" to medication.

This chapter will now consider other kinds of documents with a particular emphasis on practices of circulation, and the notion of narrative therapy as being "linking lives therapy" (apparently a term used by Michael White when considering the shortcomings of the term "narrative therapy"; Fox, personal communication).

Online documents

Many of the documents discussed in the earlier narrative literature are letters written by therapists to clients, usually summarising particularly striking segments of a therapy conversation, often with the principal intention of strengthening an emerging preferred story.

On reading *Narrative Means to Therapeutic Ends*, it is apparent how much the medium of the written word has changed since 1989. I wrote the great majority of this chapter on a smartphone, for example. Working with young adults, it is striking how much of their lives are lived online, and it is important to not fall prey to the dominant discourse among those who grew up in pre-internet times that online relationships are somehow inferior to, or not as real as, offline relationships. When working with young people with cystic fibrosis (CF)—a condition that means that face-to-face contact is strictly advised against due to the risk of cross-infection—online communications can be particularly important, though, as above, it is vital that the therapist takes ethical responsibility for the process.

I have used email to interview one young woman with CF, Sam, about self-harm—both in the "traditional" sense of cutting, but also through not taking nebulised antibiotics. She had very limited lung function and had been told that she was ineligible for a lung transplant, and was periodically overcome by a sense of despair about the impending end to her short and painful life.

My intention in interviewing her was to richly describe her knowledge about self-harm—what made it likely (including dominant gendered and ableist discourses around "normality"), the effects it had on her life, what action she could take to affect these effects, and the principles and hopes that informed these actions. It was notable that she told me in this email exchange that she had started cutting in response to experiences of sexual abuse—something she had never stated face to face. (There is some research suggesting that people feel more comfortable disclosing highly personal information online than in person; Goss & Anthony, 2003.) The composite document of questions and her responses proved helpful for her, and she referred to it at times "when despair took hold".

When asked at the end of our work if she would allow the document to be shared with other people with CF who were struggling with self-harm, she agreed. Often, when people are asked for their permission to share these kinds of documents with others experiencing similar difficulties, they tend to agree. This sense of altruism and generosity around sharing stories has been a consistent feature of narrative therapy work with people living with chronic illness and disability, and raises interesting questions about the individualising practices of confidentiality within the therapy world (see Epston & White, 1992; and Hahs & Colic, 2012, for a further exploration of these ideas).

This document was shared with Gavin, another person with CF who was self—harming. He reported at the end of our work together that reading Sam's account had been the most helpful part of the therapy. It had helped him feel that he was not alone in self-harming, and that it was something that could be lived with and not a sign that he was mad. In particular, he had been struck by the courage Sam had shown in talking frankly about her experiences of abuse, and this courage had inspired him to be open about his own emerging gay sexual identification—he felt that starting to accept and talk about this had been instrumental in leaving cutting behind.

This exemplifies the power of another's story to create the experience of resonance and to precipitate transport (White, 2007). It also highlights how dialogue is rhizomatic; conversations and connections between people can lead in entirely unexpected directions. Hence it could not have been foretold how Sam's account of stepping away from self-harm could play such a pivotal role in Gavin's coming out. Jodi Aman has written compellingly of the therapist as both a host and a guest in therapeutic relationships (2006), and circulation practices such as this extend the metaphor further. The therapist, by introducing Sam and Gavin through their documents, played a role akin to a skilled host at a party: introducing two strangers to one another and helping them connect. Gavin subsequently agreed to share some of his reflections on this process by email with Sam, who was very moved and gratified to hear about her contribution to his life. Sam sadly died within a few months of this exchange.

Whilst writing this, I had a sense that even talking about email has become outdated: many young people no longer use email, preferring various social media instead. Therapists, though, may not have yet explored opportunities for using social media as a medium for therapy. This may partly be as a result of a lack of knowledge thereof and confidence in using them, but also due to the Information Governance (IG) constraints of various organisations. It can take considerable persistence and effort to reassure senior colleagues in IG that sharing emails between patients is a manageable risk. Such practices though may not be permitted with NHS Trusts. However, seemingly, the NHS is becoming gradually less fearful of the internet, and there may be scope in the future to regularly conduct email therapy, run groups via video-conferencing platforms, or use Facebook groups for outsider witness practice.

Documents of knowledge and skills

David Epston's work with people reclaiming their lives from anorexia, in particular the idea of putting together "archives" of people's skills and knowledge in relation to particular problems (Maisel & Epston, 2004), provides a template for narrative therapy practice. An example of applying these ideas is in relation to "needle phobia"—a potentially life-threatening problem in conditions such as insulin-requiring diabetes or CF. Narrative therapists can approach this problem by seeking to uncover significant initiatives in relation to the problem ("needle-phobic" people tend to have *some* experience of successfully tolerating injections or blood tests), and to explore and richly describe these occasions, with particular emphasis on what people have done and the ethical foundation behind these acts.

Therapists can also use a similar "question and answer" email format to put together documents summarising this work. This process has many benefits. First, it provides a concrete summary of the work for the person to refer to in future. Second, it provides an account of their identity as someone with valuable knowledge and skills, someone worthy of respect. Third, it is the very process of reflection this entails that requires the person to take a step back from their lives and view themselves in an appreciative way. Fourth, it allows for the circulation of these hard-won skills and knowledges to others who might benefit. This latter consideration can have an enormously beneficial effect. Epston and White (1992) discuss this in their paper "Consulting your consultants", and they quote Mauss (1954) by way of explaining the importance of such reciprocity: "to accept without returning or repaying more is to face subordination, to become a client and subservient" (Mauss, 1954, p. 72).

An excerpt from this kind of document is shown below.

What kinds of responses have you found helpful from others (family/friends) when you are having bloods taken?

For me, it has always been great having my mum there, because we are so alike and close and she always tries to be as supporting as she can when she is there with me.

Which must be hard for her seeing me going through pain and fear. But it's just really nice to know that someone is there who I know cares. I mean when I do get scared and do have an "outburst" of fear (I think that might be the most friendly word I can think of for it) sometimes she did get angry and we would argue and for me it kinda worked a bit. It made me think how I was wasting people's time and that it could be done quickly … it made me just want to have it done with. I think for the person to be patient and understanding is a great start. Like my friend Jen was there and saw I was nervous and was just herself and just talked about general things, then when it came to it, she just gave me this big hug and told me it would be ok. Even though I was crying and so beyond scared she kept her cool, and was patient and just supporting and really helped.

How is it helpful for staff to approach taking your blood? What advice would you give to nursing/medical staff about how to do this?

Be calm? Because if you know that the patient does have these outbursts of fear and can hyperventilate, it can be very easy to think "oh god no, is this going to take three minutes or thirty?" and I totally understand this because it's a simple thing but at the same time you can really tell if a nurse is nervous about doing it and that used to put me on edge. Please don't look at us with pity, it used to be so frustrating as a teenager to be looked at with pity after the occurrence of an outburst because in my eyes I was already ashamed of what happened … and I know it's meant well but it doesn't feel that way. So my tip, be calm, no pity and also don't be a pushover. Have a no nonsense attitude, it feels in a way comforting and for me is also a reminder that you have other things to do and not all day to spend waiting for me.

On a number of occasions, sharing such a document with newly referred people with needle phobia can be the only needed contribution of the narrative therapist. The process of hearing about someone else's skills and solutions often leads to a person reconnecting with their own skills, knowledge, and solutions, as opposed to them receiving particular "advice" from others.

Collective documents

Collective documents can also be significantly instrumental in helping people move their lives in preferred directions (Boyle et al., 2003; Denborough, 2008; The Irish Blind/Wheelchair Association).

Around seven years ago, I started working one day a week in a service for people who had lost limbs. I could see very few people for therapy and was keen to reach as many people as possible to try and acknowledge the psychological impact of limb loss on people and their families, to normalise distress (in the sense of trying to help people not feel weak or crazy for feeling distressed), and to make useful suggestions about what might help. I looked online for any resources on these subjects and drew a blank. So I shared my dilemma with the service's user group and asked them if they would be happy to be interviewed about their experiences, with the intention of documenting their stories and making them available for others as leaflets. They were enthusiastic and generous in their responses, and I interviewed several of them individually around the twin themes of the effects on them of limb loss, and what they had found helpful in mitigating the negative effects.

In addition to these individual interviews, I also convened a day-long series of conversations with patients along the lines of the "sickle cell" day (Lunn, 2008) and the chapter on recording trauma testimonies in Denborough (2006) with the same essential topics. By recording discussions both in audio format and on flip-charts, post-its, etc., this information could then be used to develop leaflets, one focusing on the early stages after amputation surgery, the other on life in the longer term. These leaflets were produced *en masse*. The emphasis in the final versions was on personal narrative and multiple voices. It can be very helpful to reflect the multiplicity of experiences by providing contrasting accounts—see, for example, the following excerpt from *Living with Limb Loss: The Early Stages* about different experiences post-discharge after amputation surgery:

> I had been in hospital for three months. I was desperate to get out of the hospital, but I didn't want to meet the real world. I felt detached—as though I'd stopped and the world was going on around me. I felt my spark had gone—I was no longer me.
>
> The first thing I did when I got home was put a load of washing on—it felt great! It was a lovely day for hanging the washing out!
>
> The first thing I wanted to do was get out and go for a pint!

This emphasised the multi-storied nature of life with limb loss and prevented the formation of norms around how people "should" respond—hopefully allowing for the possibility of the experiences of resonance and transport, most commonly associated with drama, though we are no less "moved" (in White's sense of catharsis with a "k") by stories we witness through writing or images (White, 2007).

The other leaflet was *Living with Limb Loss: Getting Back on Track*, and covered a huge range of topics including ways of responding to the stares of others:

> If people look at you in your wheelchair, or with your prosthetic leg, they often don't know how to approach you—whether they are intruding, and how to talk to you. Now I lead the way—I smile at them and say "Alright mate? How you doing? Are you having a good day?" If they see you smiling, they will, nine out of ten times, smile back because you are leading the way. That definitely works, definitely.

The narrative therapist can also emphasise the "small and the ordinary" (Weingarten, 1998) exceptions to problem-saturated narratives of deficit, disability, and devaluation. Stories that aim to challenge or subvert problem stories in the realm of illness and disability can often be stories of extraordinary endurance, for example of heroism, of unattainable resilience that, despite the best of intentions, can serve to further oppress people already living with compromised physical functioning and marginalised, "spoiled" identities (Goffman, 1963). Arthur Frank has cautioned against the hazards of such stories (Frank, 2013). Hilde Lindemann-Nelson (2001) has coined the term "boomerang story" for any story that:

> re-identifies an individual who belongs to the … [marginalised/ devalued] … group, representing the person as an exception, a stand-out, different from the rest. By attempting to repair one person's identity but leaving the other members of the group untouched, the story boomerangs. It ends up reinforcing the master narrative it's trying to undermine.

(Lindemann-Nelson, 2001, p. 177)

Being engaged in this project in the aftermath of the London 2012 Paralympics was discursively a mixed blessing for amputees: they were constructed in the media as heroic athletes for whom anything is possible given sufficient grit and determination. This discourse dovetailed neatly with the Conservative government's representation of those disabled people reliant on state benefits as a reflection of individual personal failure: if these disabled people could achieve so much, what excuse did the rest have for their lives of indolent "scrounging"? For the man in his fifties with bilateral trans-tibial amputations secondary to peripheral vascular disease, type-2 diabetes, coronary heart disease, and chronic pain, such discursive constructions of heroism can be quite toxic.

Participants in the co-development of these leaflets were also keen to challenge dominant deficit-laden narratives about amputees— explicitly through the text but also, crucially, through images. They collated photos of themselves that represented preferred stories of their lives and identities—everything from one man flying a plane, another DJ-ing in a nightclub, another standing in the snow on holiday—and we included them in the leaflets. I was struck in the ensuing years by how often I had to replenish stocks of these leaflets in the reception area, and many people subsequently told me that reading these leaflets had been an important step along the way to getting life back on track following limb loss. I am indebted to all those who participated in this initiative.

Letters with pictures

Michael White has written of the importance of the images that come to mind when we bear witness to the stories of people's lives and the sense of resonance and reverberation that can be triggered (2007, 2011). In my experiences of being in a supervision group that used an outsider witness framework, it is the images, the visual metaphors, that were expressed in the outsider witnesses' reflections that have been the most salient. It seems as though there is something particularly memorable about a visual image. If written documents are to some extent about rendering the ephemeral permanent, then surely it is a good idea to include images in them, and indeed many practitioners are exploring diverse ways of doing this (see Cheryl White, 2011; Epilogue: Continuing Conversations, for a summary).

Particularly with Google's Image Search function (other search engines are available!), it is very easy and quick to find suitable images to include in a letter or other document. For example, I was working with a young woman who had a rather "all or nothing approach" to her management of a serious chronic illness. After a couple of conversations, we developed an externalised description of her different approaches to her condition, personifying them as two stereotypical characters: New York Business Woman and Californian Surf Dude. New York Businesswoman got up at 5.30 am and hit the gym hard prior to working twelve-hour days. She took a very punitive, ascetic approach to her life and her body, but got everything done on time and was super-organised. Californian Surf Dude was so laid back, she was practically horizontal, "mañana" her byword. This was a useful externalisation in that it introduced some much-needed humour into what was a fairly grim situation and, crucially, reduced the young woman's susceptibility to self-blame. At one point, I knew I was not going to be seeing her for some time and was keen to keep the externalised storyline going, to prompt her reflection, and just to let her know I was thinking of her, I sent her the letter below:

Hi Merry,
Wondered if you'd seen these characters recently?

(Image inserted of a)   (Image inserted of a)
New York Business Woman   **Californian Surf Dude**
If you're interested, I'd be keen to hear more about them both:

- When they first appeared in your life?
- What influence they have had on your life—positive and/or negative?
- What support systems do they both rely on? Who, in your life now or in the past, are their friends and supporters?
- How do they work? What tactics do they use to influence you?
- How do you feel about them both? Do you want more or less of them in your life? Why?

I'm sure I'll think of some more questions when we meet again, so that will do for now.

I look forward to seeing you.
Rob

This document took less than five minutes to put together, including having to work out how to crop the image of the surfer, and prompted Merry to engage in considerable reflection prior to the next session.

Documents for healthcare staff

When illness enters people's lives and starts to dominate, it changes the social landscape of the person. Often, relationships within the workplace (and I would include many of the relationships within the work of childcare—the teachers, other parents at school, pick-up times etc.—in this definition) become less prominent as illness saps energy, limits mobility, and reduces the reliability of the body.

Simultaneously, other relationships become imbued with vital significance—in acute care, or early diagnostic stages, life can hinge on communications with healthcare staff; as illness becomes chronic, rehabilitation teams come to populate life in ways that friends, colleagues, and acquaintances used to. The geographical spread of a person's significant relationships can diminish markedly—a person's social circle reduces dramatically in diameter, often to the extent that almost all of the people a person knows might well be employed in the same organisation. While this is a complex emotional experience for people—they often resent the fact that they are forced into these relationships at the expense of others, and have feelings of love as well as hatred and envy towards the healthcare staff involved in their lives—the fact that the social and relational context of the person has become so limited and so local is an opportunity for the narrative therapist. The smaller and more parochial the person's social world, the easier it is for us as clinicians to influence the stories that circulate about the person. If we can help often just a handful of key healthcare staff to bear witness to preferred accounts of the life and identity of the person, then we can exert a significant effect on their social context in ways that would be much harder with more distributed social networks of people whose lives encompass home, work, sports, and pastimes.

The following is an example of a document co-written with a woman, Jan, who was dying on the CF ward. She had been relatively well then had a sudden downturn in her respiratory function due to a pulmonary embolism. She was referred in relation to panic attacks which were triggered by the slightest exertion due to her very minimal lung capacity. As the problem was discussed, it became clear that the well-intentioned reactions of others were not helping, so within a session a guidance document was co-written and circulated among her family and the ward staff. In part, it explained a little about panic attacks—a combination of my outsider professional knowledge and her insider knowledge. It then went on to summarise some of the things Jan had found helpful to do when panic struck, including putting her head up and looking at the ceiling. This was probably something to do with opening up her airways, or perhaps just a distraction, but either way it was decided to at least make it a bit more enjoyable—hence a picture of a muscular celebrity she fancied was pinned to the ceiling to provide a focal point. The rest of the document was Jan's advice to staff:

Things that staff can do:

1. Stay with her. This is the key thing that helps.
2. Don't touch her/hold her hand unless she asks/indicates that she wants you to do this.
3. Say things like:
   a. "You're going to be alright."
   b. "You're alright—you can breathe."

    c. "Nothing's going to happen to you."
    d. "You'll be ok again in a few minutes."
  4. Don't say things that might be confrontational like:
    a. "It's only a panic attack."
    b. "You've got to calm down."
  5. Don't freak out. Staying calm is really important, even when you
     don't feel it. Be reassured that people don't die of panic attacks
     and that this will pass within ten minutes maximum.

This will probably help Jan recover. She will then move to Phase
Two. In this stage, Jan finds it helpful to:

  1. Lie down in the foetal position on her bed and cuddle a pillow.
  2. Continue trying to get her breathing back into a normal steady
     rhythm.

In this stage, Jan finds it helpful for staff to try and distract her. Telling
her something funny is often helpful—making her laugh. If you are
struggling to think of anything, please use the joke book provided*.

Jan has never had a panic attack that has lasted longer than ten
minutes, so stay with her. Afterwards, Jan is likely to feel on edge for
a while, then gradually emotional and drained. If you have to go off
and leave her, please make plans to come back and see her when you
can, and try not to forget.

**Thanks for reading this—any questions, speak to Jan or Rob
(psychologist)**

(*The joke book I picked up cheaply online—it wasn't even slightly
funny, but in a way that made it all the funnier!)

This letter had a very positive effect—all relevant staff read it and
their behaviour changed accordingly in a very short space of time,
and despite the very low levels of nursing cover, particularly at night.
Jan was very appreciative of how nursing staff responded to her episodes of panic and breathlessness which continued until her death
two weeks later. Clearly, it is important in a letter like this to consider
how it too constructs staff members as well as the person. If the point
of the letter is to encourage staff members to approach things in a
different way, it is prudent to guard against them feeling criticised or
patronised: invite them into the position of the caring and competent

professional; acknowledging how relentlessly busy they are is only fair too.

Emphasising agency is important in written communications to teams—modern healthcare requires patients to strike a delicate balance between passive obedience and taking action. If patients are not seen as helping themselves then they can be in for a rough ride. In cases of poor adherence to medication regimes, it can be hugely influential to emphasise in documents (and of course "case discussions") stories of people struggling on to do their best despite very trying circumstances.

Letter-writing campaigns

Sometimes it can be helpful to reach further out into people's social networks. I worked with Joy for several years. Rather like Jan above, Joy had grown up with CF—a chronic illness that imposed all kinds of limits on her life and required her to engage in increasingly complex and arduous self-management. Joy's experience was that she was resented for this by her parents and she was cruelly bullied by them, and emotionally, physically, and financially abused throughout her life. Alcohol provided an escape. As she got older and more poorly, particularly after she was told she was ineligible for the lung transplant list, she became very tired and found it increasingly hard to resist the stories that her parents still told of her: that she was selfish, had never amounted to much, that she wasn't a good enough daughter. She felt very alone within her marriage and her husband was violent towards her; she was similarly susceptible to the notion that she was not a good enough wife. She was troubled by self-blame and guilt. At times, she was overtaken by a sense of emptiness, a notion that her life was and had always been futile.

Much of my work with Joy involved breaking from the dominance of the story that her parents and husband had recruited her into, and tracing other stories of her life and identity that contributed to more of a sense that she was a woman of value, someone whose life had been worthwhile. Documents played a large part in our work—in part, these served as *aides memoire* as we did not meet often and Joy's respiratory function was so low that repeated infections had compromised her brain function, so she found it hard to remember our conversations—ideal conditions for the old story to reassert its dominance in her life.

Many of the documents were simple (highly edited) summaries of sessions, though at times we co-wrote other documents such as a list of excuses she could make when her mother rang and started to criticise her or harass her for money: Joy kept these on the fridge for quick reference. At times, I gave her documents to read that reflected some of our work—for example, Joy Syfer's (1971) humorous feminist essay "Why I want a wife". The most memorable documents for both of us, however, were the responses we received from letters I wrote to several people who had known Joy through her early life. Stephen Madigan (2011) describes such "letter-writing campaigns" where the therapist writes a letter (such as the one below) and sends it to people who know the person in order to reinforce the preferred counter-story, to reconnect the person with the treasured relationships of their lives, and to invite some re-membering practices in relation to these people.

Dear Friend of Joy's
My name is Rob Whittaker and I am a Clinical Psychologist in the Adult Cystic Fibrosis Unit in Leeds, UK.

Joy and I have been meeting for some time and we have decided that I should write to you so that I might solicit your support. As you are probably aware, Joy has endured a lot of difficulties in her life, not least of which she has been living with cystic fibrosis and the various challenges this involves. Joy has also told me about some people in her life who have compounded these difficulties, through a lack of support or a lack of understanding for her situation.

However, Joy has also told me about some very significant people in her life, who have been tremendously important to her, providing her with emotional sustenance over the years and helping shape her sense of herself as a person of worth and value—Joy's "community of concern".

I am writing to ask if you could please send a brief letter to me at the above address expressing:

  a. How you remember your history with Joy—what memories you have of her and what it has been like for you to know her.
  b. Your thoughts and feelings about Joy's responses to the difficulties of her life and what kind of a woman she is in your estimation.

c. How you would like to see your relationship with Joy develop
   in future.

Joy and I will then read the letter together in one of our meetings. We
hope that your letter of support is not too much to ask, and we want
you to know it will be greatly appreciated. Thanks in advance with
this and my very best wishes.

Dr. Rob Whittaker
Clinical Psychologist

All four of the recipients replied with great thought and care, sharing
personal reminiscences of Joy and particularly the contribution she had
made to their lives. For example, Kay, who met Joy while doing work
experience at a school at the age seventeen and had never seen her
since, though they had become pen-pals. Now in her mid-forties, Kay
wrote in her letter "Joy is a wonderful person and she inspired me to
train to be a teacher after completing my A Levels". She reflected on
some of the hard times in her own life, with a daughter with learning difficulties and how "Joy's letters have supported me a great deal,
always full of empathy despite having a difficult time herself ... I am
privileged to know her". Kath wrote of how she had got to know Joy as
a little girl when she was in her class at primary school. She made fond
references to the ever-changing colour of Joy's hair, and to Joy "never
moaning ... never introspective, and even when she told me that nothing more ... could be done, there was no self-pity but she looked to the
future when she hoped 'to be less tired and to do more' ... even though
we are far apart my thoughts are often of her". A final quote, this time
from Sylvia:

I first met Joy when, with her father, she managed our garden.
My husband loved having her around as he could "rib" her
about her very black hair. He always thought she was a great
kid and I think was very fond of her. I just liked having her
around, she worked hard even on her not so good days. I don't
think her father appreciated her enthusiasm for work. She was
bubbly and fun. Never took advantage of our friendship. She
approached her illness as if it was just one of those things,
never dwelling on it, in fact it was many years before I realised
what she had.

All these letters were addressed to me (Joy's choice), and Joy decided that once I had them all back I should read them aloud so we both heard them at the same time. It was enormously moving for both of us. As our conversations progressed, she continued to have a very challenging time, both with the ever-increasing effects of CF on her life as well as the ongoing unpleasantness that characterised her family relationships. She nonetheless developed some effective ways of responding to these difficulties, and she told me that the emphasis in our work on her bottom-line values and preferences in terms of relationships had been instrumental.

At the end of our work together, I was keen to do what I could to try and increase the longevity and health of her preferred story about herself. To this end, I gathered all of the documents that had been so central in our time together, and Joy kindly agreed to be interviewed about them so that I and others could learn from her experiences.

ROB: Of all the letters and documents here, which are the most important to you?

JOY: These (indicates the responses to the letter-writing campaign letter)

ROB: What particularly sticks in your mind about those?

JOY: How lovely they all are—I can't believe they are talking about me … I find it difficult to read them only because I'm not very good at praising myself. I don't think I have done anything special, I don't think I've done anything untoward or inspiring, I am just me, so the letters are very difficult to read, but they are the ones I wouldn't ever want to throw away. I do quietly now and again read them when things are getting me down a bit.

ROB: At what points might you go and get them out?

JOY: Times when I feel that I'm on my own. I do feel sometimes as though I'm all alone in the world … With my parents as they are, it's nice to think there are people out there who care about me.

ROB: So these letters are important to you and you return to them for a sort of "top-up dose", a reminder about what's positive about these relationships and that you are part of a network of people who very genuinely care for you?

JOY: These people are not caring for my CF—they are knowing Joy for Joy. They know I have CF, but CF isn't at the forefront of their mind in the way that it is at the hospital.

ROB: You read these and you are reconnecting with these relationships that are not CF-free but where CF isn't the focus?

JOY: Yes—and that's how I've always wanted to live my life. I never wanted CF to be at the forefront of my mind ... But yeah when there's times when I feel quite low and I just need to reconnect things, it's just nice to read them. I don't think I could read all three of them at once though—I'd probably just pick one and read that—because they are so emotional to read.

ROB: Yes.

JOY: Writing something down is quite powerful ... in a letter, you can go over it again and again and get a more powerful response than just talking. Somehow things sound more genuine when they are written down ...

ROB: Of these other letters, the ones I have sent you, what sticks out?

JOY: The ones about my Mum—they are really powerful, even now two years on. If I start thinking that it's all just me, that it's all my fault what my parents did and that I deserve it—there's one sentence in here on your opinion—that you think I "have been treated in ways that are appalling and utterly unfair". Now if I read that I start thinking no it's not all my fault, if any of it's my fault at all. There are still some bits of me that think that I could have done things better, but reading through these letters makes me think that, no, I am quite a nice person and not at all what my family make me out to be.

Formal letters to other agencies

It is sometimes the case that the difficulties that people are experiencing might be better addressed in another service. For example, in working with people with chronic pain, at times it is helpful to refer onto colleagues in community mental health services who might be better placed to help with problems relating to ongoing effects of abuse in childhood. Or in work with an HIV-positive man recently who was struggling with an m-cat addiction, it was agreed that it would be most helpful for him to seek the advice and support of a local drug and alcohol service. In these cases, it is unfortunately necessary to engage in deficit-laden accounts of the person's life and identity—unless these documents conform to linguistic traditions of pathologisation and categorisation, then they do not meet the intake criteria for the recipient services. Regrettably, it is my experience that this is more and more the case; perhaps due to decreasing budgets in public-sector services and the resultant "raising the bar" in terms of referral criteria as a way of managing referral numbers.

Some years ago, I wrote a letter for a man I had been seeing in relation to difficulties adhering to his CF medication regime, and in the course of our work he told me about experiences of abuse in childhood: we spent some time talking about the ongoing effects of this abuse and his responses to these. Our work included him telling the story of how he had been punished for his illness in childhood, how he had been humiliated, physically abused, and shamed for his physical limitations as a young boy and the inconvenience this had caused his family. I was influenced in these conversations by the idea of double listening, and much of our work was focused on tracing his small acts of defiance against his parents' abusive behaviour and charting the relational history of the values and principles that provided a foundation for this resistance, and working these into an alternative storyline of his life and identity that he found more sustaining and hopeful.

Prior to the conclusion to this work, however, I left my post, and we agreed that I refer him on to the psychological therapies service within his local mental health agency. I duly wrote a letter emphasising his traumatic past, his depression, flashbacks, distress, obsessional behaviours, etc. and sent him a copy too. Next time I saw him, he thanked me for doing the letter but said "you forgot to put what a top bloke I am!".

Since then, if I ever have to write this kind of letter, I discuss openly my concerns with the person and let them know that I am telling their story in such terms for a specific purpose, not because I believe it to be a valid or helpful way of thinking about them. In the event that they request a copy of the letter, I will enclose a compliment slip where I affirm the strategic nature of the letter, distance myself from its depiction of the person, and let them know what a top bloke/lass I think they are.

And finally

There are no real conclusions to this chapter—other than to reiterate my hope that it might have inspired you to engage with and further develop ways of using the written word within narrative practice.

I end with a reflection on the importance of the written word to me. Over the years, I have kept a file of all those cards, letters, and even poems I have received from patients over the years—a very touching testimony to the relationships I have shared with them. Rather like Joy, at times when I perhaps need it most, I find myself seeking out this file and being touched by their, often simple, acknowledgement of what our conversations and my presence has meant to them, and it reconnects me with what is important to me about this work and helps me carry on.

References

Aman, J. (2006). Therapist as host: making my guests feel welcome. *International Journal of Narrative Therapy and Community Work, 3*: 3–10.

Boyle, B., Clancy, A., Connolly, A., Hefferman, B., Howley, E., Keena, M., Lang, D., McSharry, M., Moloney, G., Morrell, S., Murphy, C., Murphy, N., Murphy, T., Murtagh, M., Murray, L., Murray, P., Oulton, K., Richards, A., O'Riordan, J., Roche, D., Smyth, R., Tomrey, A., Walsh, P., & Daly, E. (2003). The same in difference: the work of the Peer Counsellors of the Irish Wheelchair Association and the National Council for the Blind of Ireland. *International Journal of Narrative Therapy and Community Work, 2*: 4–16.

Denborough, D. (2006). *Trauma: Narrative Responses to Traumatic Experience.* Adelaide: Dulwich Centre Publications.

Denborough, D. (2008). *Collective Narrative Practice: Responding to Individuals, Groups and Communities Who Have Experienced Trauma.* Adelaide: Dulwich Centre Publications.

Duval, J., & Beres, L. (2011). *Innovations in Narrative Therapy: Connecting Practice, Training and Research.* London: W. W. Norton.

Epston, D. (1994). Extending the conversation. *Family Therapy Networker, 18*: 31–37.

Epston, D., & White, M. (1992). *Experience, Contradiction, Narrative and Imagination.* Adelaide: Dulwich Centre Publications.

Fox, H. (2003). Using therapeutic documents: a review. *International Journal of Narrative Therapy and Community Work, 4*: 25–35.

Frank, A. (2013). The necessity and dangers of illness narratives, especially at the end of life. In: Y. Gunaratnem & D. Oliviere (Eds.), *Narrative and Stories in Health Care* (pp. 161–176). Oxford: Oxford University Press.

Goffman, E. (1963). *Stigma: Notes on the Management of Spoiled Identity.* New York: Simon & Schuster.

Goss, A., & Anthony, K. (2003). *Technology in Counselling and Psychotherapy: A Practitioner's Guide*. London: Palgrave MacMillan.

Hahs, A., & Colic, M. (2012). Reducing collusion with individualism and dichotomous thinking in counselling. *International Journal of Narrative Therapy and Community Work*, 3: 11–17.

Lindemann-Nelson, H. (2001). *Damaged Identities, Narrative Repair*. London: Cornell University Press.

Lunn, S. (2008). Spreading the news: coping tricks from the sickle cell clinic. *International Journal of Narrative Therapy and Community Work*, 3: 41–46.

Madigan, S. (2011). *Narrative Therapy: Psychotherapy Series*. Washington, DC: APA.

Maisel, R., & Epston, D. (2004). *Biting the Hand that Starves You: Inspiring Resistance to Anorexia/Bulimia*. New York: W. W. Norton.

Mann, S. (2002). Collaborative representation: narrative ideas in practice. *Gecko: A Journal of Deconstruction and Narrative Ideas in Therapeutic Practice*, 2: 39–49.

Mauss, M. (1954). *The Gift: Forms and Functions of Exchange in Archaic Societies*. London: Cohen & West.

Morgan, A. (2006). The position of the therapist in working with children and their families. In: M. White & A. Morgan (Eds.), *Narrative Therapy with Children and Their Families* (pp. 57–84). Adelaide: Dulwich Centre Publications.

Parry, A., & Doan, R. E. (1994). *Story Revisions: Narrative Therapy in the Postmodern World*. New York: Guilford Press.

Syfer, J. (1971). Why I want a wife. *Ms. Magazine*. https://www.uic.edu/orgs/cwluherstory/CWLUArchive/wantawife.html (accessed 11 March).

Weingarten, K. (1998). The small and the ordinary: the daily practice of a post-modern narrative therapy. *Family Process*, 37: 3–15.

White, C. (2011). Epilogue: continuing conversations. In: M. White (Ed.), *Narrative Practice: Continuing the Conversation* (pp. 157–180). New York: W. W. Norton.

White, M. (1997). *Narratives of Therapists' Lives*. Adelaide: Dulwich Centre Publications.

White, M. (2007). *Maps of Narrative Practice*. London: W. W. Norton.

White, M. (2011). *Narrative Practice: Continuing the Conversation*. New York: W. W. Norton.

White, M. & Epston, D. (1990). *Narrative Means to Therapeutic Ends*. New York: W. W. Norton.

White, M., & Morgan, A. (2006). *Narrative Therapy with Children and Their Families*. Adelaide: Dulwich Centre Publications.

Wilson, J. (1998). *Child-Focused Practice: A Collaborative Systemic Approach*. London: Karnac.

GLOSSARY

Absent but implicit: The premise that any description of a life experience can only be understood by discerning what the expression/description *is* from what it *is not*. That which it is not, or that to which it is in contrast, is referred to as the absent but implicit.

Agency: The perception or realisation that a person can have some control or choice in the direction that their life takes.

Alternative story: A story that develops in counselling that speaks of something different to what the dominant story or problematic account presents about a person or their actions.

Co-authoring: A co-joint process whereby the person and their therapist develop alternative stories together.

Collective documents: The practice by which responses (written/visual) from many people are gathered, and then assembled to form one document.

Consulting your consultants: The process by which a therapist consults a person about the knowledge they have, for example, about living with a particular health concern or problem; this knowledge can then be passed on or distributed to others in some way.

Co-research: The practice by which people are invited to become research partners with the people undertaking the study rather than being "studied" themselves; this process encourages all to join together to research what is known about the problem and ways to respond.

Decentred/Centred positioning: Where the worker seeks to privilege the preferences, knowledges, and skills of the person, as opposed to those of the therapist or their therapeutic model.

Deconstruction: The process of unpacking the meaning of something; this could be a term, phrase, idea, norm, or even discourse. The intention of doing so is to avoid making assumptions based upon any wider social understandings/meanings available to a person, and instead seek to explore the particular meaning/s for the person in relation to their personal context.

Discourse: A set of ideas, beliefs, meanings, or representations developed by society and that suggest a particular way of being, doing, or understanding.

Dominant story/discourse: An understanding of a situation, subject, or problem based upon ideas that have been developed within a particular social, historical, and cultural context, and acknowledging that such stories shape how people make sense of, and act within, their lives.

Double listening: Listening out for what an expression is not, as well as what it is. Thus hearing that anger may also reflect something that has been disregarded, oppressed, or devalued.

Editorialising: The practice by which a therapist records then reflects back a number of salient points or steps that a person has been making. This can encourage a person to reflect on this action, or series of actions, and what it may mean for them.

Experience near descriptions: Descriptions of events/meanings that move from the "broad" to the "local" and "personal"; what a situation means for a person and their context.

Externalising conversations: Practices by which a therapist facilitates a process of viewing a problem as separate to the person; thus a person and problem are viewed in relationship to one another, as opposed to a problem being seen as within a person.

Landscape of action/Landscape of identity: The landscape of action constitutes the story material of a unique outcome (a person's concrete experiences: what happened and in what way), whereas the landscape of identity illustrates how developing a preferred story (from unique outcomes) can also enable a renegotiation of how a person views their identity.

Multi-storied: The belief that one story may never fully encompass a person's complexity of thought, actions, feelings, or experiences—rather, people are considered to be "multi-storied".

Mutual influence questions: Questions that explore the symbiotic relationship between the person and the problem; i.e., not only how the problem affects the person, but also how the person affects the problem.

Naturalistic/Structuralistic descriptions: Naturalistic descriptions are explanations which describe problems as "truths" about a person's "nature", "character", or "self". Structuralistic descriptions locate problems within people.

Outsider witnessing practices: The means by which people are brought together in some way (either physically present or virtual) in order to witness and respond to a re-telling of events/a story.

Positioning: A term used to describe a conscious and deliberate re-negotiation of a particular relationship, for example, with a person, a problem, a discourse or norm; a person therefore considers how much importance (or the meaning) they wish to give to a particular idea, and their reasons for this.

Postmodernism: A philosophical movement that aims to critically examine assumptions that are a part of the established "truths" of society.

Practices of circulation: The many means and methods by which preferred stories, knowledge, or skills may be distributed to others, usually in order to support the "thickening" process.

Problem exploration: The process by which concerns that a person brings to a worker are unpacked; this may include exploring why this feels like a problem for a person, the effects of the problem, and what kind of relationship to a problem a person would prefer to have.

Problem-saturated stories: These are stories often heard in therapy that dominate and provide little room or scope for alternative stories about a person's lived experience to be heard.

Re-authoring: A process in narrative therapy whereby the therapist and person co-create an alternative preferred story or stories.

Relational ethics: A way of situating and recognising ethical action explicitly within the relationship and context, encouraging a worker to consider ethics on a decision-by-decision basis.

Re-membering practices: Involves facilitating a process of "re-viewing" how a person perceives their relationships with themselves and with others, in relation to preferred directions or possibilities in their life.

Resonance: The experience of a person's life having similarities to another's (or the therapist's), particularly in terms of what the person gives value to.

Scaffolding: The process by which therapists use questions to bridge the gap between what is known and familiar about a problem (to the person), and what is unfamiliar but possible to know, and relates to knowledge of preferred possibilities in a person's life.

Shoulds to Coulds Map: A map developed by Walther, Redstone, and Holmgren that provides a scaffold for exploring and deconstructing norms and discourse.

Social constructionism: Argues that perceptions or meanings about reality are developed by our interactions, communications, and experiences with others and with society.

Statement of Position Map One (SOPM1): A map developed by Michael White that supports workers with problem exploration.

Statement of Position Map Two (SOPM2): A map developed by Michael White that supports workers to develop and thicken unique outcomes.

Story: A description of events that are linked over time, within context, and according to a particular plot or theme.

Structuralism/Non-structuralism: Structuralism refers to the belief that those things around us, including ourselves, are made up of structures that can be studied and understood—and the "truth" or "reality" accessed in some way. Non-structuralism believes that reality is a social construction and, therefore, fluid and ever-evolving through our interactions with one another.

Testimony: A written or spoken account of events/a story.

Thick descriptions: Thick refers to rich descriptions, for example, detailed and thorough explanations or descriptions of events/experiences. However, this is not just in relation to what (concretely) may have occurred, but rather what such actions may mean for a person, so rich in detail and meaning.

Thickening: Refers to the process by which, through storying and developing meaning around an event, situation, relationship, hope, etc., it may become more richly described and visible to a person.

Thin descriptions: By contrast, refer to explanations with little exploration, detail, or meaning. Frequently, thin may refer to broad descriptions that may have been applied to a person or problem without further unpacking, or consideration of a person's unique context.

Unique outcomes/exceptions/initiatives/sparkling moments: Are examples or stories about experiences, responses, or acts that are recognised as exceptions to the problem story in that they are seen to speak of something different.

Visibility: A term used to describe an intentional "bringing into awareness" by a therapist or person; for example, to bring into awareness ideas that may be influencing what a person feels they "should" be doing, or what is known about a problem.

Witnessing/Re-telling: The practice by which other people are recruited or invited to hear a person telling their story, often in a particular way. This practice can be undertaken with other people present (outsider witnessing), or indirectly through the use of letters or documents that are circulated to others, with the option for resonances or responses to be collated and fed back to a person.

INDEX